Grounded

Also by Dallas Ann H. Erwood

WWII Notebook & Letters

2020 Words of Pandemic Poetry

60 Shades of Steno A Memoir

GROUNDED

Poetry by Dallas Ann H. Erwood

Drawings by Eileen Gianguzi

Published by AquaZebra Book Publishing
Cathedral City, CA

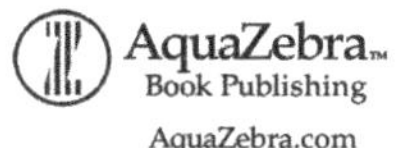

First Edition

Erwood, Dallas Ann H.
Grounded

Library of Congress Control Number: 2023901571

ISBN 978-1-954604-99-5 (paperback)

Cover and interior illustrations by Eileen Gianguzi

Design & Layout
Mark E. Anderson

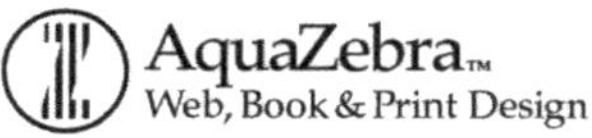

www.aquazebra.com

Printed in the United States of America

Dedicated to:

Our July 22 boys, Charlie & Rick

Table of Contents

Table of Illustrations

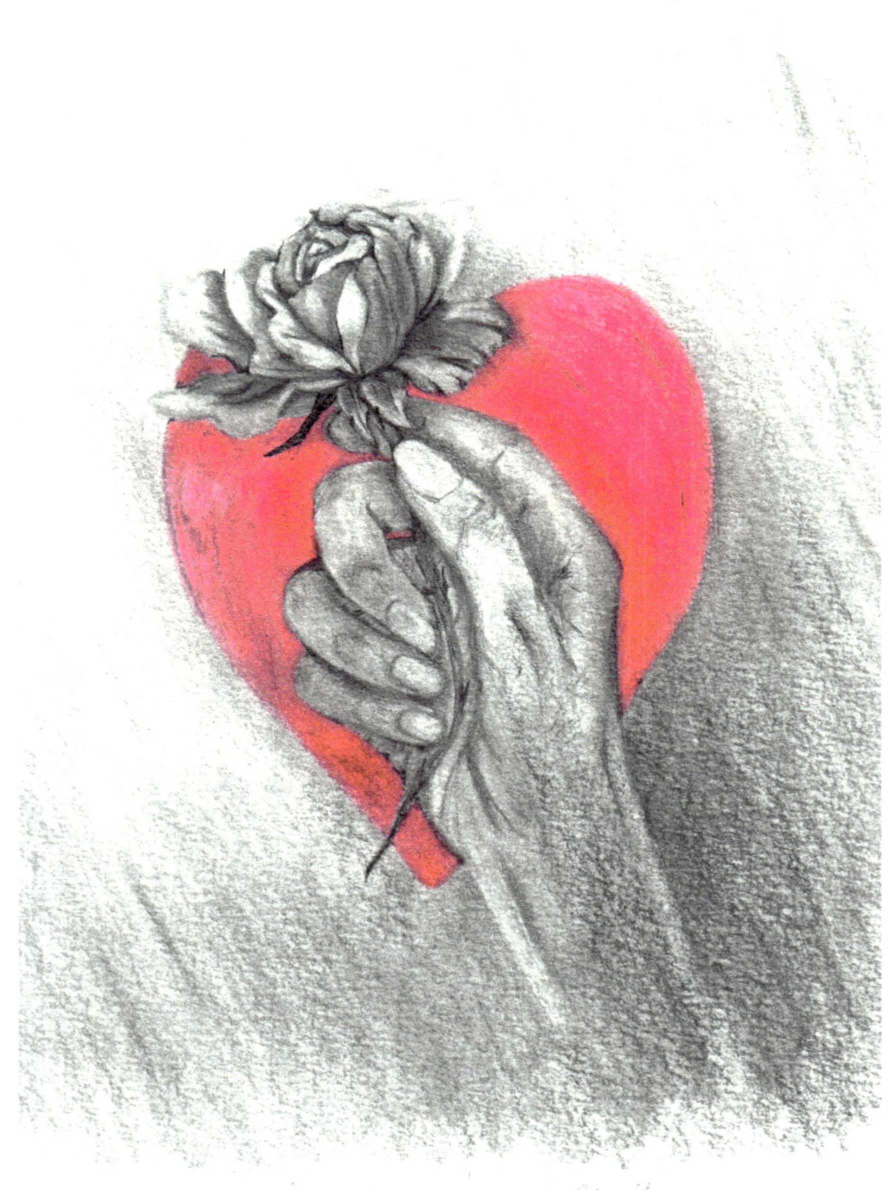

Chapter One

My Love

Hi, Darlin'

Hi, Darlin' D.A.,
Sweet man of my dreams!
Could this relationship
Really be what it seems?

It feels so fantastic,
The stuff dreams are made on,
All the love we can make
From morning till dawn.

I'm one lucky girl
To live in this world,
So grateful and good
And true, as it should

Be loving and strong,
Healthy and long,
Feet moving free
You loving me.

Rick E.

He's a little bit shy
But, oh, so cute!
Could this be the guy?
I think I'll relearn the flute.

When we're together
I get so nervous
Because I know
He's here for a purpose.

The purpose is Love,
But the feeling is fear.
Please take over the feeling
And let the purpose come near.

Because life's too short
To live in the past.
Give me today with you,
And I'll make it last

Forever!

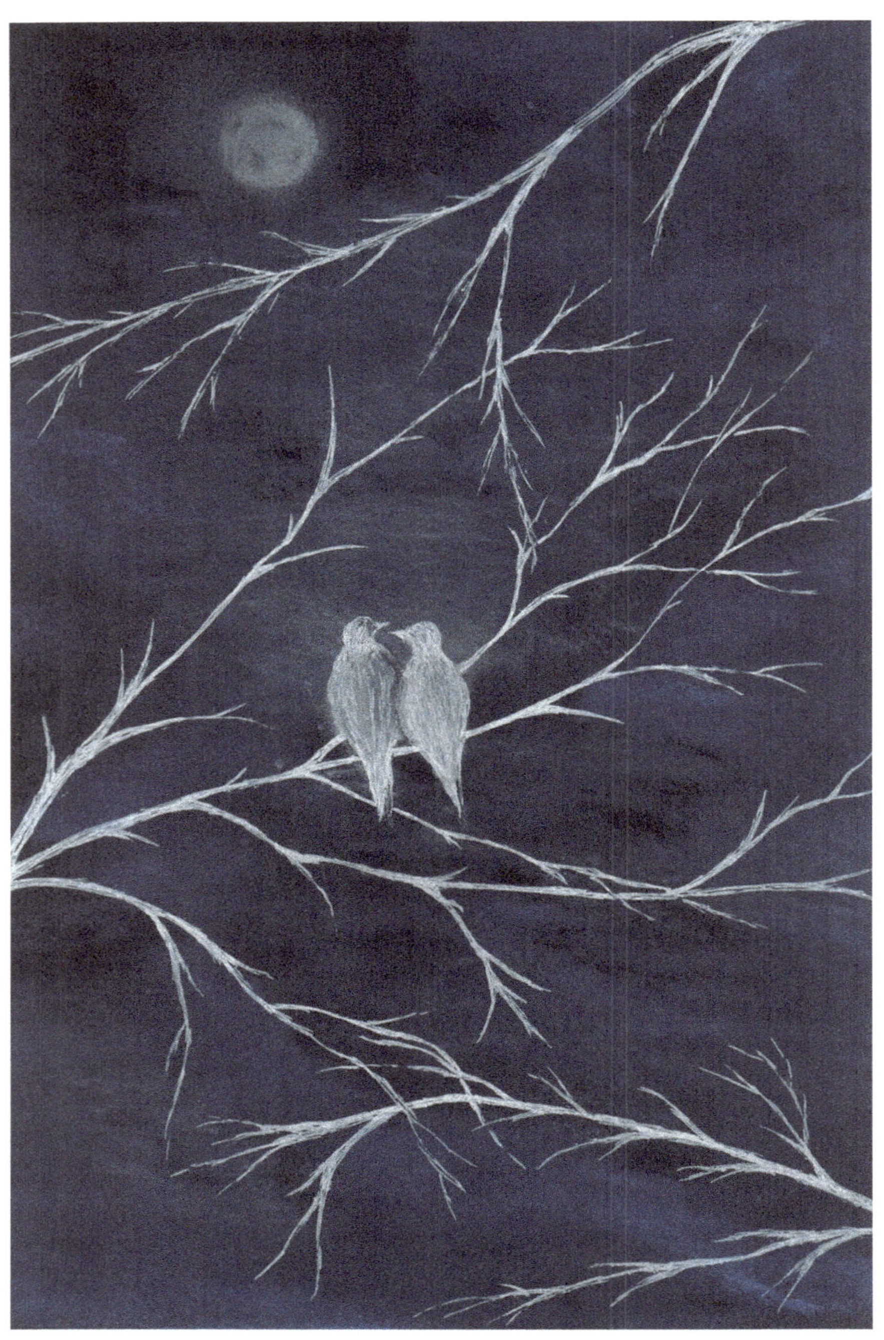

A Night Full of Love

Nineteen-eighty-nine, the tenth day of June,
A day for marrying two children of the moon,
With poetry and roses and romantic bliss,
Resolutions and vows confirmed with a kiss.

Rubies and diamonds for Dallas and Rick,
A night full of Love to light the wick.
With God on our side and Love as his name,
We'll have what it takes to sustain the flame.

Family and friends, near and far,
Future children, whoever you are,
Thank you for coming, enjoy your stay
And wish us luck as we go on our way . . .

. . . for what we are to see remains
A mystery of joys and pains
Without each other we could not bear,
But together we are a perfect pair.

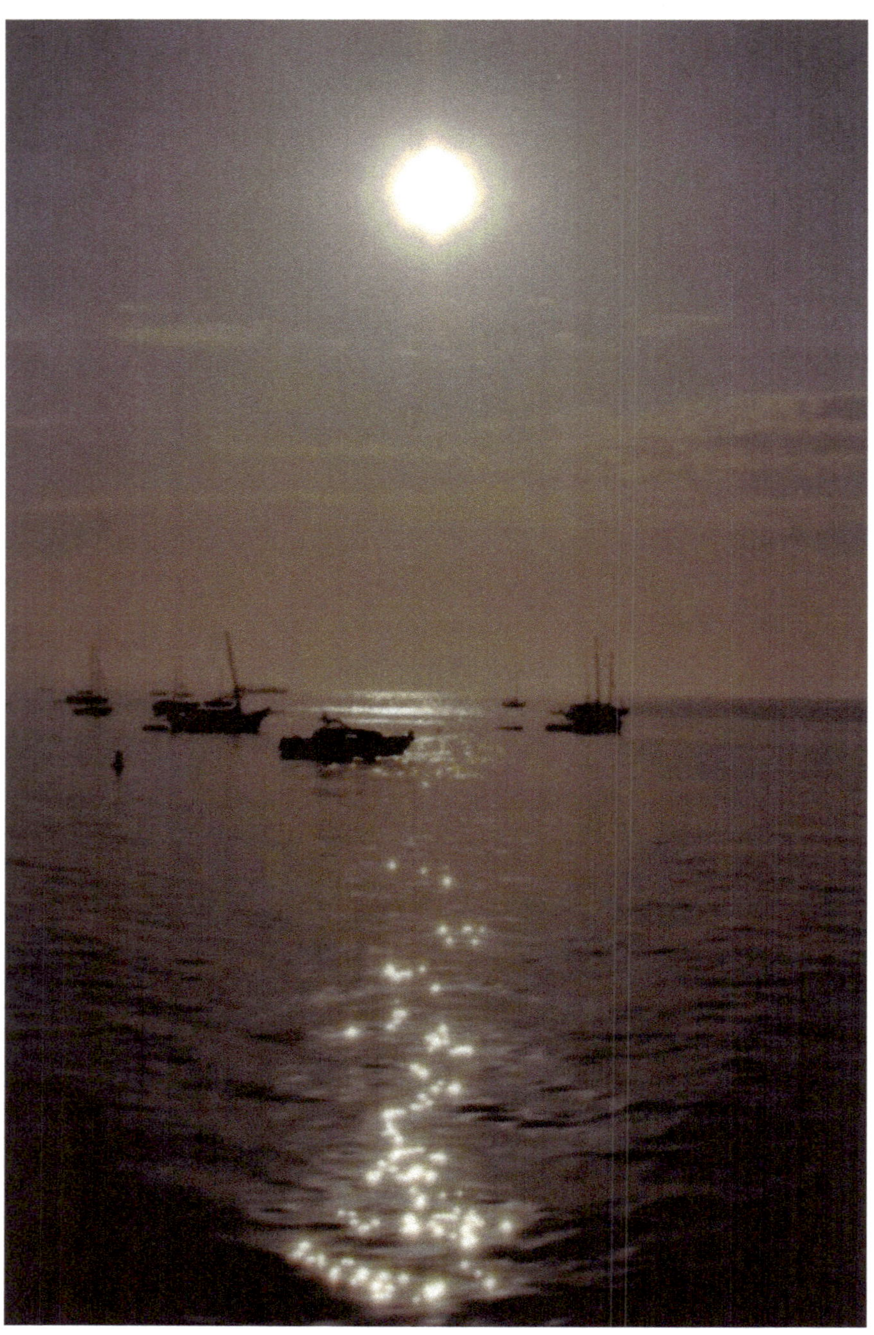

It's Time

It's time for us to intermingle,
Get tangled up until we tingle.
A love like ours, so tried and true,
I want to share my life with you.

Yesterday has come and gone
And tomorrow has yet to dawn
Let's seize today before it's known
Never again to be alone.

The decision to marry wasn't made overnight,
But never has a decision felt so right.
Always know that I will care for you
As long as the sky and sea are blue.

So here's to you, my partner for life,
As we become husband and wife,
When the sun sets at day's end,
I'll spend each night with my best friend!

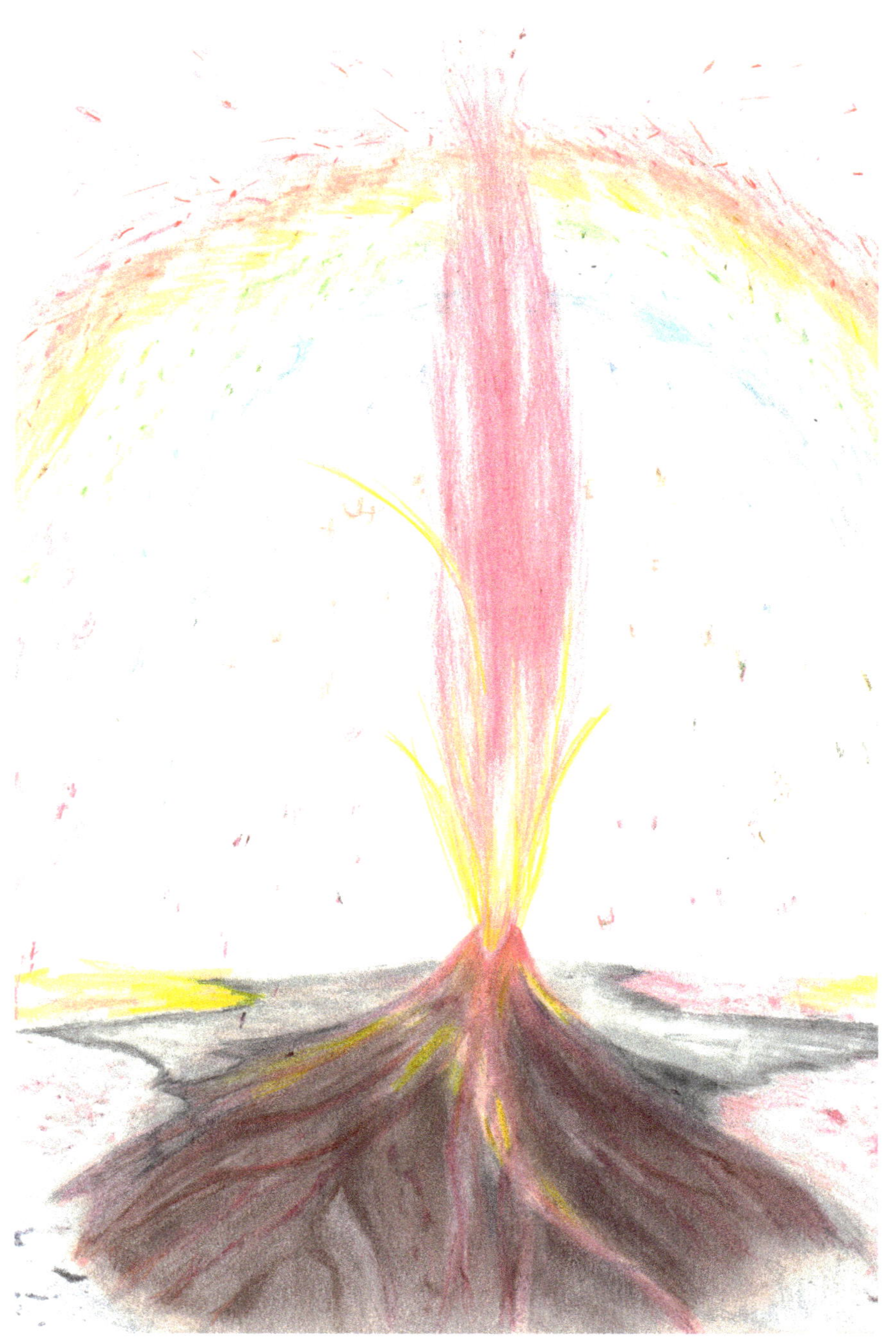

Mount Saint Heavens

Our wedding was like a volcano:
Bubbling, erupting, there she blows!
Red-hot lava full of love
Shot up to the heavens above.

Our guests numbered 227
And the cake was a spiral toward heaven
The "E" cake-topper was four feet tall
I wonder, did we eat it all?

When the judge began his litany
That's when it finally hit me
Hard as a ton of bricks:
Rick was mine & I was Rick's.

Remembering our beautiful bash
I see a rainbow of pastel ash,
It's falling from heaven with grace
Creating a rock-solid base.

Honeymoon

Off they went to Maine
To spend their honeymoon.
They'll never be the same
Once lain upon the dune.

He said, "It's 6:00 o'clock,
And what are we to do?"
She said, "Let's take a walk,
My darling, sweet baboo."

Poetry is the key
And laughter is the door,
Youth is the melody
They'll sing forevermore.

What a gracious gift
Bestowed upon their heart
The stairway gives them lift
Oh, what a lovely start!

Sunrise

Sunrise, sunrise,
See the color of his eyes.
I've never seen such pretty skies
Or felt so many heady highs!

Sunset, sunset,
Oh, how his scorn makes me upset.
I must be feeling marital fret.
Time for a heartfelt tête-à-tête.

Raindrops, rainbow,
First I'm high, then I'm low.
I want to stay. I want to go.
I'll be your friend and ne'er your foe.

Love's lost, love's found.
Losers, weepers all around.
Let's get our feet back on the ground
And revel in what beauty's bound!

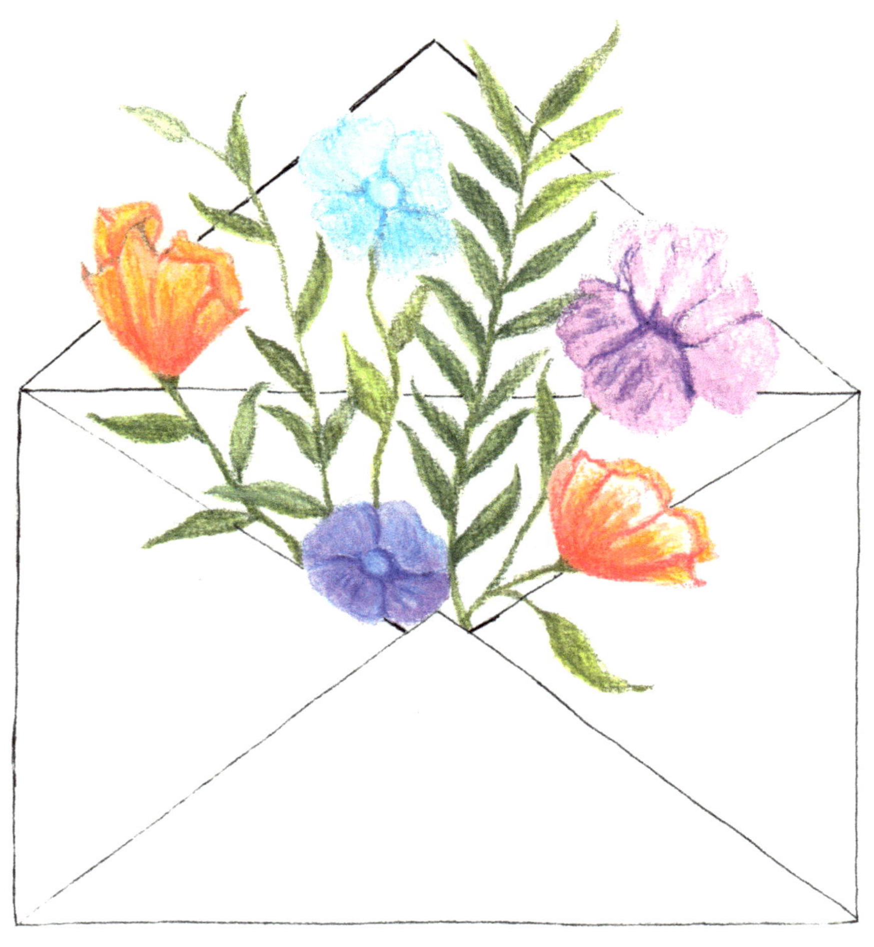

1/8/2021

Thank-You Note

We had a lot of fun
On our honeymoon,
But never as much fun
As in the Romeo and Juliet room!

Here's three dollars
For the recipes,
The rest is for
Gratuities.

The island fun
Was bountiful!
Your hospitality
Was wonderful!

We'd stay all summer,
If we could.
Yours very truly,
Mr. and Mrs. Erwood.

My Love

Mornings with you
Waking up
In our room
Are golden

Watching the day
Turn to blue-green
Sorcery
I love you

When the pillow
Hits my head
And the sun sets red
I'm with you

Then at night
The moon glows white
And I'm sleeping right
Next to you.

My Old Love

My freckles used to be sweet speckles,
Now they're big aging sun spots!
My smile used to be bright white;
Now it most certainly is not!

My neck used to be long and supple,
Now it looks like a hundred year old turtle!
My love used to be a raging inferno,
Now it's warm and eternal.

My workdays now are so long,
But my old love is still strong!
My incidents of falling are more frequent,
I'm saying more often, "Sorry, I just can't."

Less messes to clean up after,
A more enriching chapter,
Friendships finer all the time
And an old love who is patient and kind.

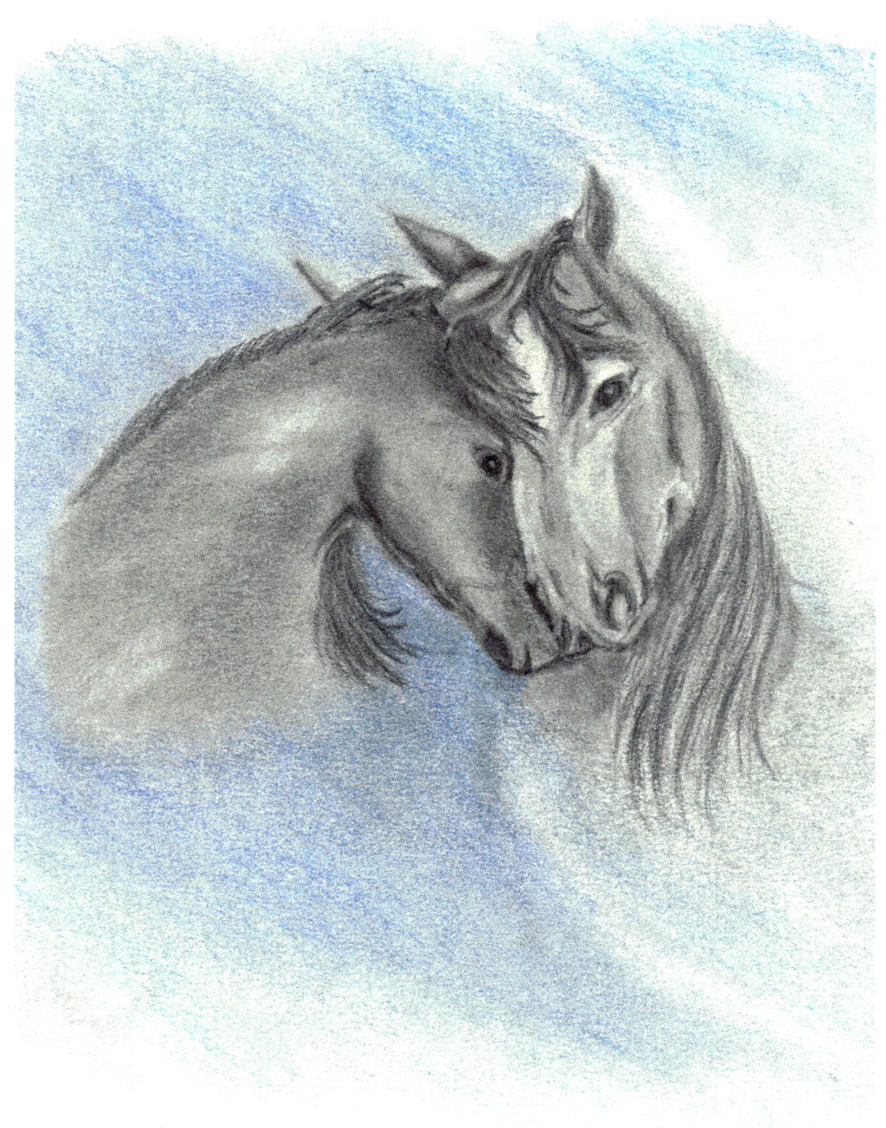

Anniversary Sonnet

He's the helium to her gravity,
The anchor to her levity.
He's the medicine for her condition,
The bookmark in her edition.

He's her hand to hold in flight,
The compass on their hike.
He's the sun to her moon,
The stable to her swoon.

He's the funny to her smart,
The honey to her tart.
He's the truth to her power,
The fruit to her flower.

He's the straight to her curly,
The late to her early.
He's the tissue to her tears,
The wonder to her years.

Anniversary Sonnet (Continued)

You're the chamomile to my calm,
The dad to my mom.
You're the light to my night,
The left to my right.

You're the love to my crush,
The polépolé to my rush.
You're the desert to my hot,
The thinker to my thought.

You're the "Kibo" to my Serengeti,
The meatball to my spaghetti.
You're the milk to my tea,
The black to my coffee.

He's the hook to my eye,
The blue to my sky.
He's the husband to my wife,
The love to my life.

What It Takes

Bottom-line love
takes a
top-of-the-line man.

No rules,
expectations;
just loving
salutations.

My dear,
sweet heart,
true love
from the start.

Kiss here,
A kiss there.
In love
Everywhere.

Impatience

God, honey, I can hardly wait
Till your flight connects with its gate
1141 flight United
When I see you, I'll be so delighted!

I can't get over the emotion of wanting
Your body near mine; it's almost haunting
Your arms and legs, so warm, so hairy
The feeling I have is definitely scary!

A crush of love stronger than desire,
Higher than a kite, hotter than fire
Raging out of control, racing with fate.
God, honey, I can hardly wait!

Marriage is a creation
Two lovers' maturation
From joy, through love, to peace
Will you try to be patient, please!

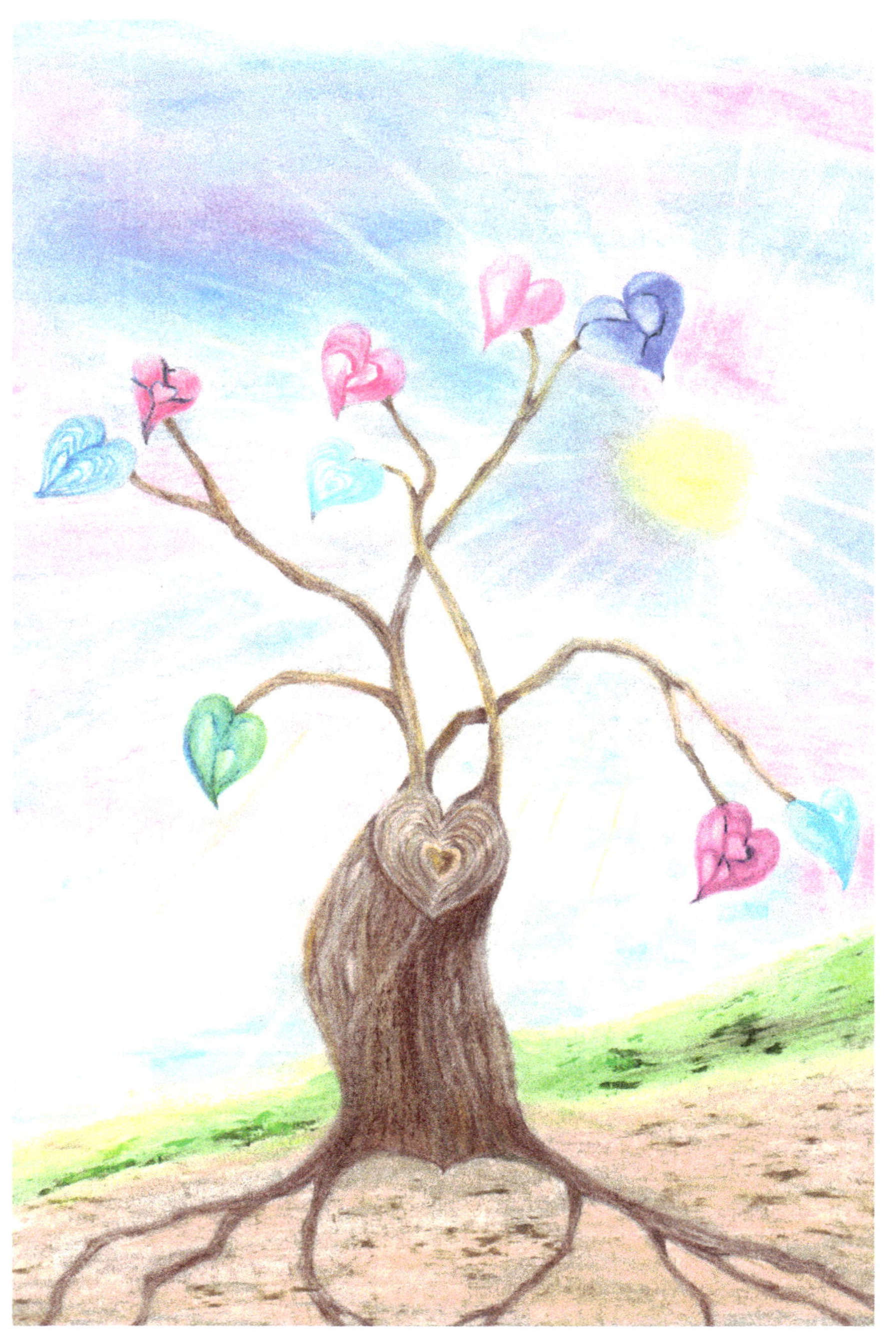

Chapter Two

Family Tree

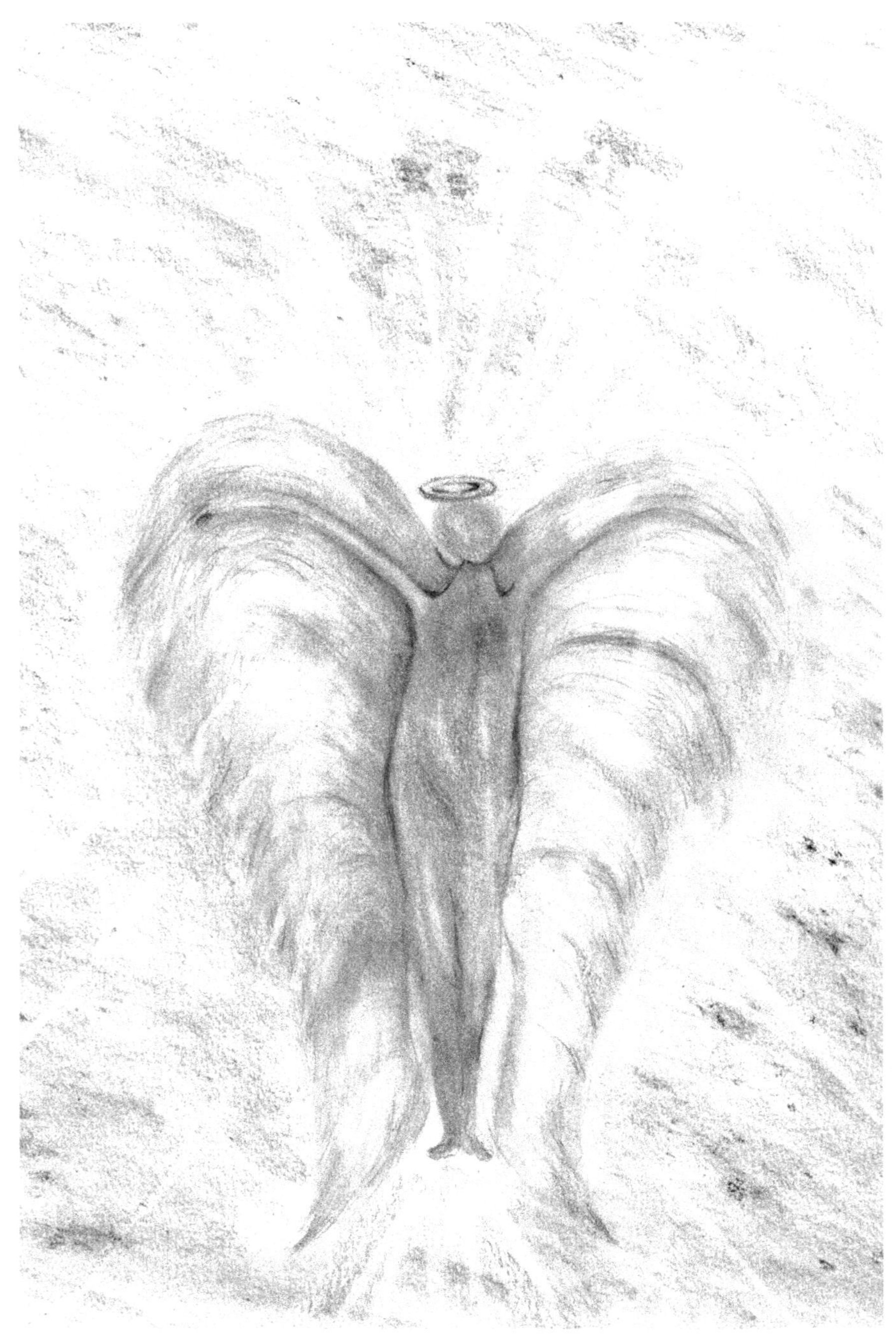

The Day My Dad Died

On the day my Dad died
All the Angels cried.

On the day my Dad appeared
All the Angels cheered.

On the day my Dad flew
Through the pearly gates of heaven

Was the day my Dad's grief and sin
Were gracefully forgiven.

Amen

When Mourning Came

Oh, God,
Daddy Dearest.
You taught.
How tender fear is.

Loving you,
Caring, too,
As I do,
I miss you.

Old trees,
Dead leaves,
Cold breeze,
Heart freeze.

New life!
I am a wife!
I have new eyes!
No more disguise!

Dad Only Knows

There are some things that Dad only knows,
Like where that cold draft is coming from,
Or where the sports page went to;

There are some things that Dad only knows,
Like Faulkner and Hemingway and San Diego State;

There are some things that Dad only knows,
Like when his daughter is burning the candle at both ends.

But there are some things that God only knows,
Like when life starts and when life ends.

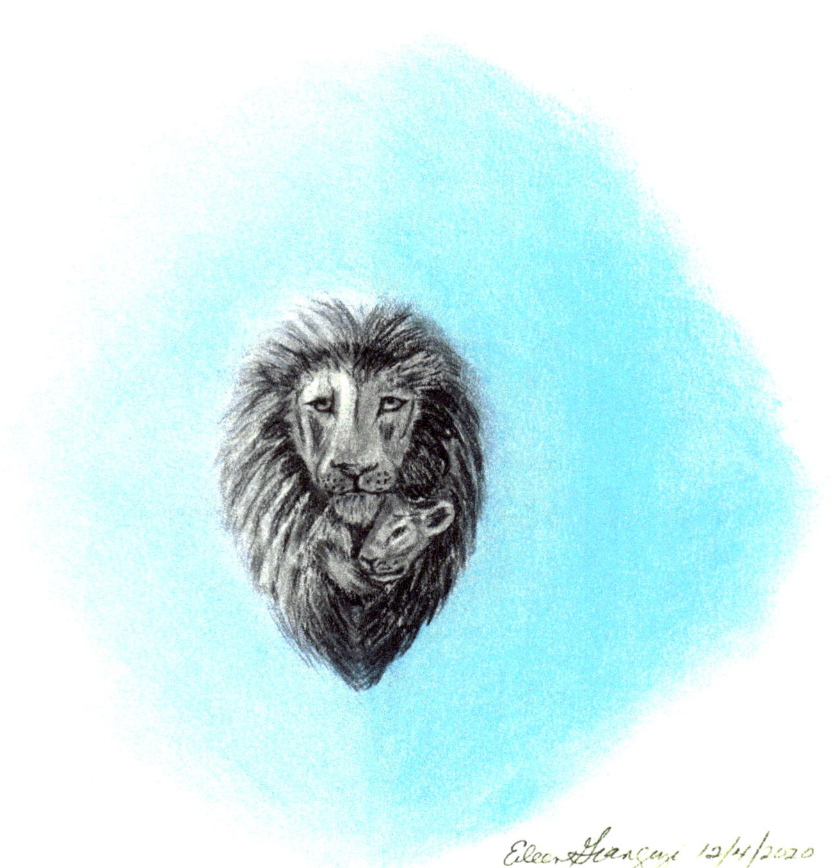
12/4/2020

What My Dad Would Say To Me Now

Stay proud
Stay strong
Stay loving
Stay long

Stand tall
Persevere
Stay together
Come here!

Be good
Behave
Be quiet
Be safe

Keep your
Head down!
Play well
Don't frown.

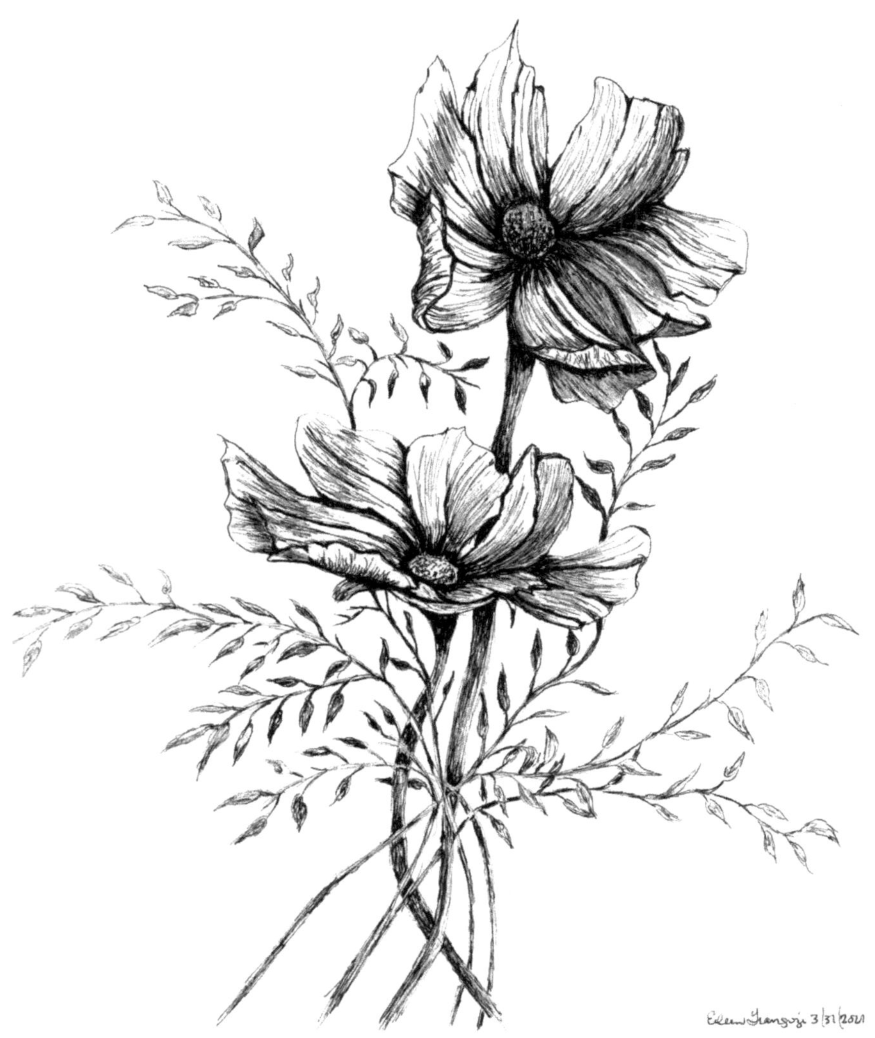

Nancy And D. Ann

Alone she is so quiet
While the howling wind outbreaks,
Sleep is a seething riot
She feels as her heart shakes.

Once when I was younger
I thought I heard her cry,
Through all our pain and hunger
I did not ask her why.

Knock and you shall enter
Her warm and glorious home
Where love is hot and tender
And abounds and heartily roams.

Together we are a pair
Ever-connected at the heart.
Emotions and a nose we share,
Mother and daughter from the start.

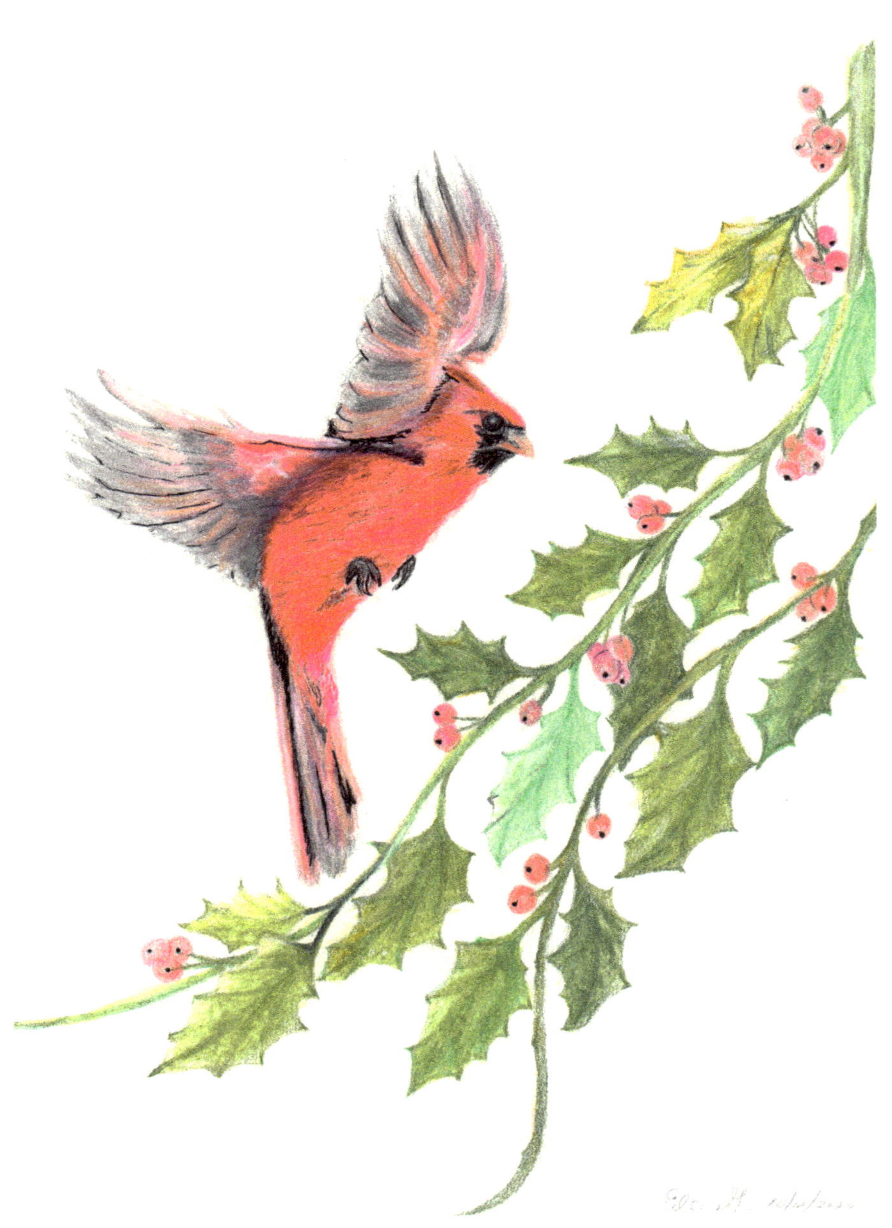

Believe

Holly Berry, bright light of our day!
I want you to make all this pain go away.
Just turn on that smile and light up that mouth
And tell us what life is really all about.

I missed you so much today, I can't stand it!
Your mother is wise; your dad a blessed bandit!
We love you so very much, our little Berry!
You're making this sad Christmas so very merry.

Take care, little girl,
And remember, don't pout!
And Santa Claus will tell you
What death's all about.

Forever Hillary

There's nothing like being Daddy's baby girl.
Take it from me, my darling Hillary.
A Love so strong it transcends this world.
And so you will see, oh sweet Hillary.

I wish you a life that's rife with success
And humility, good-natured Hillary.
May peace and happiness be your bequests
For all eternity, oh lovable Hillary.

May you hear the earth's music and sing the world's song
In perfect harmony, oh precious Hillary.
May you nights be cozy, your days be long
And absolutely free, oh beautiful Hillary.

May your sense of adventure be tempered with care
And integrity, flirtatious Hillary.
If ever you need us, we'll always be there.
And so it will be, forever Hillary.

Blame

It was the tree
That flustered me
I did not see
That great big tree

It was his mom
Who was all wrong
The love's all gone
Because of Mom

It was my dad
Who made me mad
I was so sad
Because of Dad

We put the blame
On any name.
Oh, what a shame
It is to blame!

The Mother Of Me

I love
The Mother of me.
In heaven
I'm sure
A throne
Is for her
Waiting,
Waiting,
Patiently
For the
Mother of me.

Where is
The Father of me?
In heaven
No doubt
I can
Live without
The necessity
Of the
Father of me.

Where is
The Husband of me?
By my side
Surrounding me
With love and joy
My baby boy
Eternally
The Husband
Of me.

Where is
The God of me?
Up and down,
All around,
In and out.
Without a doubt
My creator.
What's greater
Than the
God of me?

Mask Makers

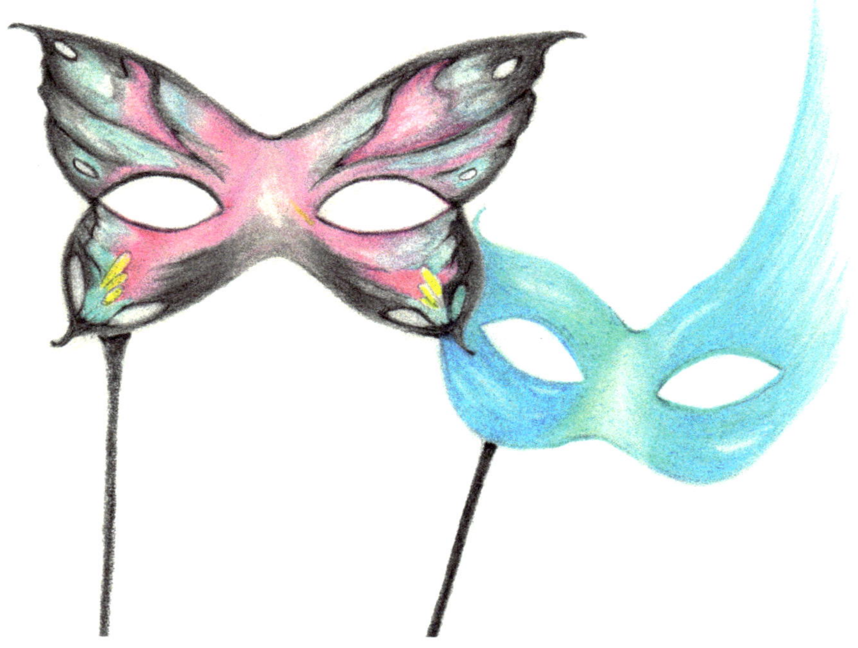

Once upon a time

There was wide-eyed wonder & smiles

Real love

Gimme a hug

Stand back!

Making masks!!

Greasy loving hands,

Pale pretty faces.

My friends
Actually sat still for this.

Fan her dry
With a paper plate,
Get her high
On the winds of fate

Cheryl Ann, my friend
My sister, Jennie B.
Pretty baby Brin,
Baby face Hillary

Your angel is showing!!!
Terri & Holly wrote me a poem.
I believe we are reflections
Of those who would surround us.

And she is worth it.

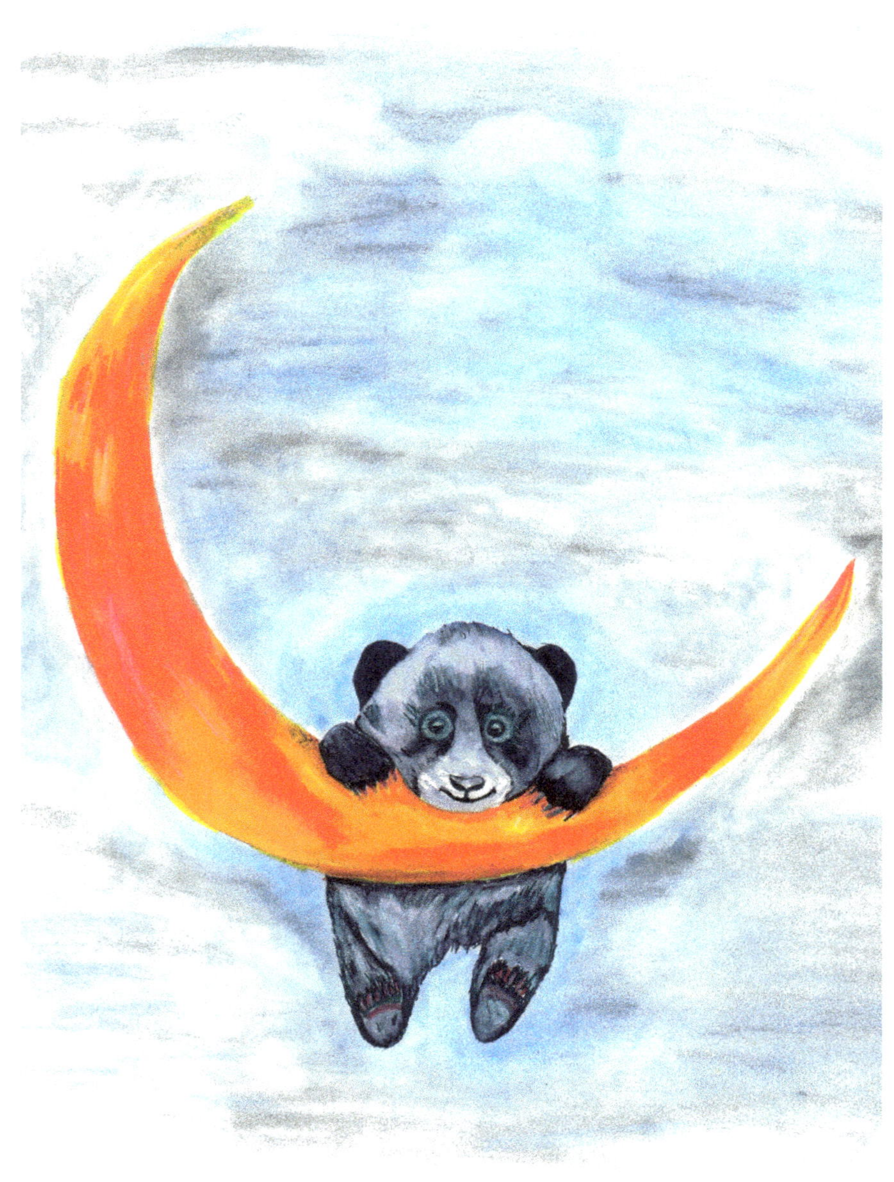

Baby Grant

Happy Birthday, Baby Grant
From your uncle and your aunt.
We missed you so much when you were here.
We love you very much, our dear.

One hundred dollars for the day
When you're eighteen and fly away.
But for today, our baby boy:
You've brought this family so much joy!

Ask mom and dad about airplanes,
And all of life's most wonderful things.
Share with your siblings all you can,
They'll grow up to be your biggest fan!

We wish you luck and happiness,
I hope and pray for all the best!
For you, for us, your uncle and aunt.
God bless you, darling boy, Baby Grant.

Melody

Miss Melo
In the yellow dress
Backlit by the sunset

Violet, orange
And the whitish-pink gleam
Of your sunscreen

Reddish hair
And skin so pretty
Time doesn't care

What counts is
The sum of your heart
And the strum of your soul

C'mon
Miss Melo
Let's rock and roll

I Love Lou

I love Lou
I love Lou
I love Lou

Curlicue
Derring-do
Loves me too

Eyes of brown
Take me down
Where I drown

Sensitive
Loves to live
And let live

I love Lou
I love Lou
I love Lou

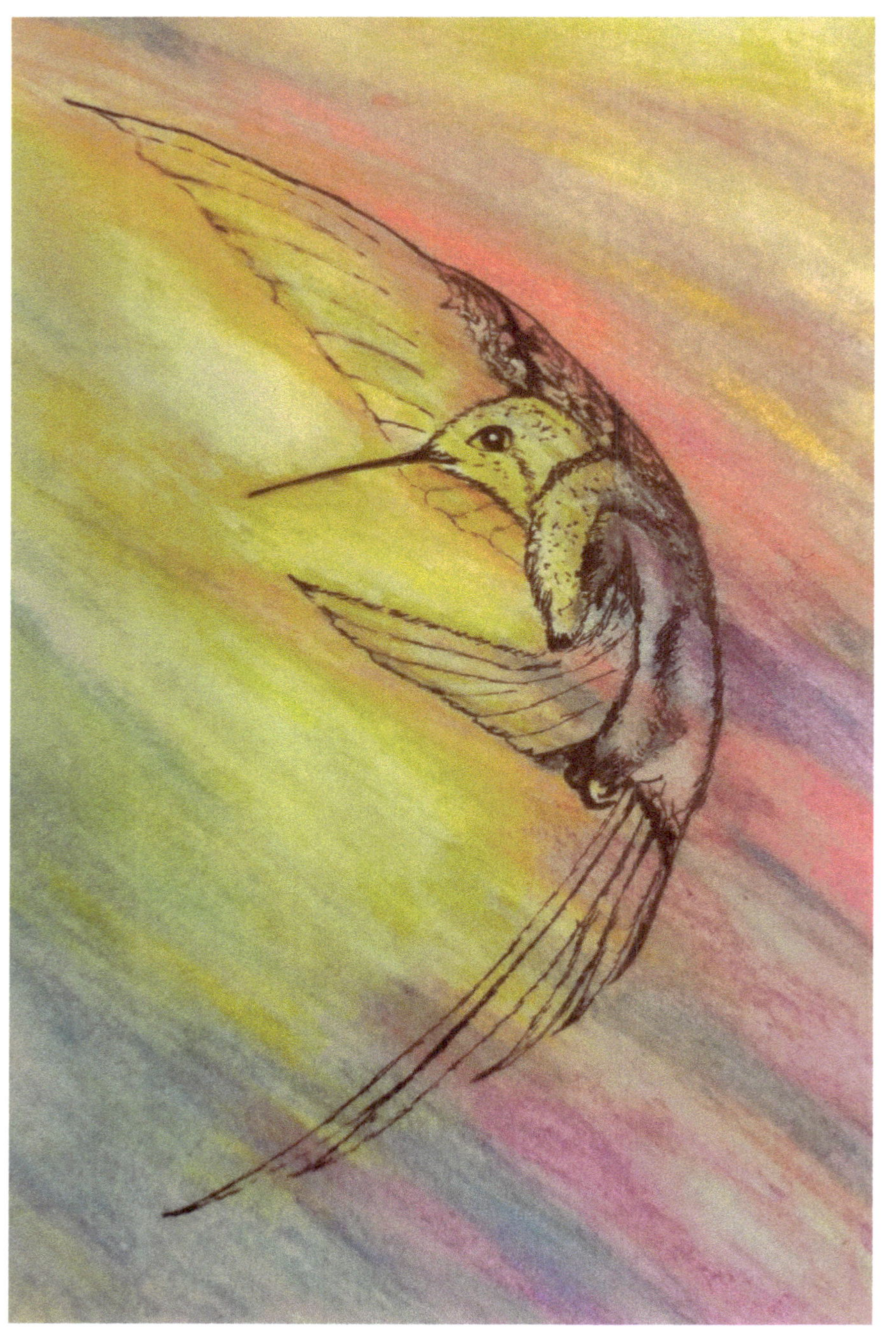

Ariane's Aura

Reds, yellows, blues, greens,
What a brilliant sight!
Talks, whispers, mumbles, screams,
Sounding out the light.

Always listening, always there
Regardless of the fright.
Iridescent dark brown hair
Longer than the night.

Without you near to see at whim
And tell me it's all right,
Nowadays I lean on Him
To climb the mountain's height.

So shine on, sis, and thank you for
Inspiring these words I write.
I couldn't, if I tried, love you more
For your aura, oh so bright!

Happy Birthday Lon

"Older than dirt,"
Those are his words!
70 years on earth
Happy day of your birth!!

A man of the land
He lends his hand
To a sister in need
To complete our dad's screed

A cherub's face
A golfer's pace
Walking with purpose
Under the cumulus

A cool golf coach
I love you so much!!!
Happy birthday, fellow cancer,
My big brother, the grass dancer.

Study In Toby

Study in Toby
A boy beauty
A big brother
My man mother

Found a photo
From a long time ago
At a fair photo booth
When you were chaperone

For me and my little friends
Tere and Patti
You would attend us
& pretend defend us

Born in February
An Aquarius baby
My North Star
With such a big heart

Toby

I have a brother I love so much
He's a stargazer and things as such
He wants to discover where we are
His eyes contain my favorite star.

He's a writer, poet, scholar and inventor
Our father was his special mentor
And now that Dad has passed away
He accompanies Mom every day.

With a heart of gold and eyes gray-green
The most searching eyes I've ever seen,
Long tawny hair and a stature so tall,
When his arms surround me I feel like a doll.

We have in common our German, our love,
Our unending quest for what's above.
There's a special place in my heart for him,
A place for visiting again and again.

Gratitude For Geoff

Dear brother,
Superstar,
Serenity's there
Within your heart.

Patience and humility
Are stronger than before.
We are all so glad to see
Your fortitude galore!

Your good nature
And emotional reserve
Are all about change
And lots of hard work.

But you got this!
From your Dada sis
Just between us
You spruce up nice!

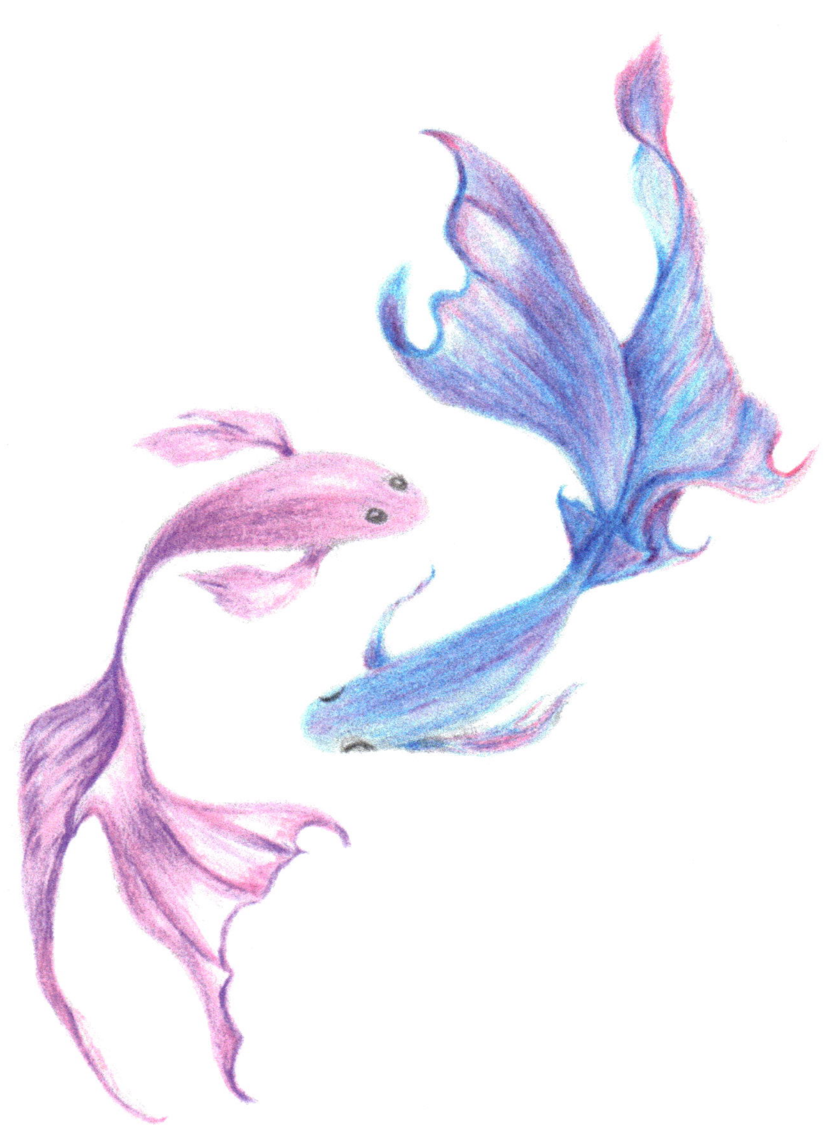

My Fishy Sister

My sister Jenn,
My Pisces Queen,
The prettiest Pisces
I've ever seen.

Her eyes are lime green,
Wise beyond seeing.
Her voice is my home
Saying, "Go to your room."

She swims with big fish!
Her command is my wish.
Hi there big sis,
What did I miss?

Blond & beautiful,
Strong & dutiful;
Accordingly,
Living her destiny.

Barnaby Dane

Here's to Karen Ann and Barnaby Dane
Who happened to meet upon an airplane:
May you never alight
From the love that took flight
The moment you asked, "So, what's your name?"

Barney's clever old friend, Richard,
Always wanting to have the last word,
Came up with an alternative quip;

Instead of, "So, what's your name?"
Barney really said this, was his claim:
"Are you going to eat that last potato chip?"

All the big laughs and love!
Hawaii at 18 and 21!!
My homecoming court escort
In a turquoise ruffled shirt and sport coat!!!

Now they're actually grandparents!
Back in the house built by our parents!!

Welcome home after 45 years!!!

It's great having your heart so near.

Rowan

Rowan O.

Roro

Gorgeous soul

Be still

My heart

And just know

First Easter

I held him

So close

Stand strong

As a tall

Rowan oak

Starting A Family

Starting a family
Hillary & Joe
Ever so happily
Building a home

Holly & Louie
Louis & Melody
Totally get me
Living in harmony

Joel & Shannon
Remind me of Michigan
One of my favorite places
In the whole nation

Ariana & Dimitri
A summer Saturday
Late June 2020
Wed for eternity

She looked like a goddess
In her white wedding dress
He looked like a prince,
Her bluebird of happiness

Weekend With Beau

Baby blue eyes
Ticklish thighs
He's all about smiles
& loves to wave "Hi!"

From sleepy-time cries
To Here Comes The Sunrise
He's such a grand child
The very best kind

He crawls down the halls
Pushed down the picture walls
Trying to stand tall
He's our babydoll

We said our good-byes
In the Sunday sunbeams
These family ties
Are all my life's dreams

Homesick

Home from Chicago
Searching for my soul
Left it in Dallas
Where cowgirls kick ass!

Morning in Utah
Mourning our youth
Laughing at laugh lines
Long in the tooth!

Home in San Diego
Finding my soul
Pomegranate party
Where everybody's artsy

I miss Mom
& Dad too
I miss you
& love you too!

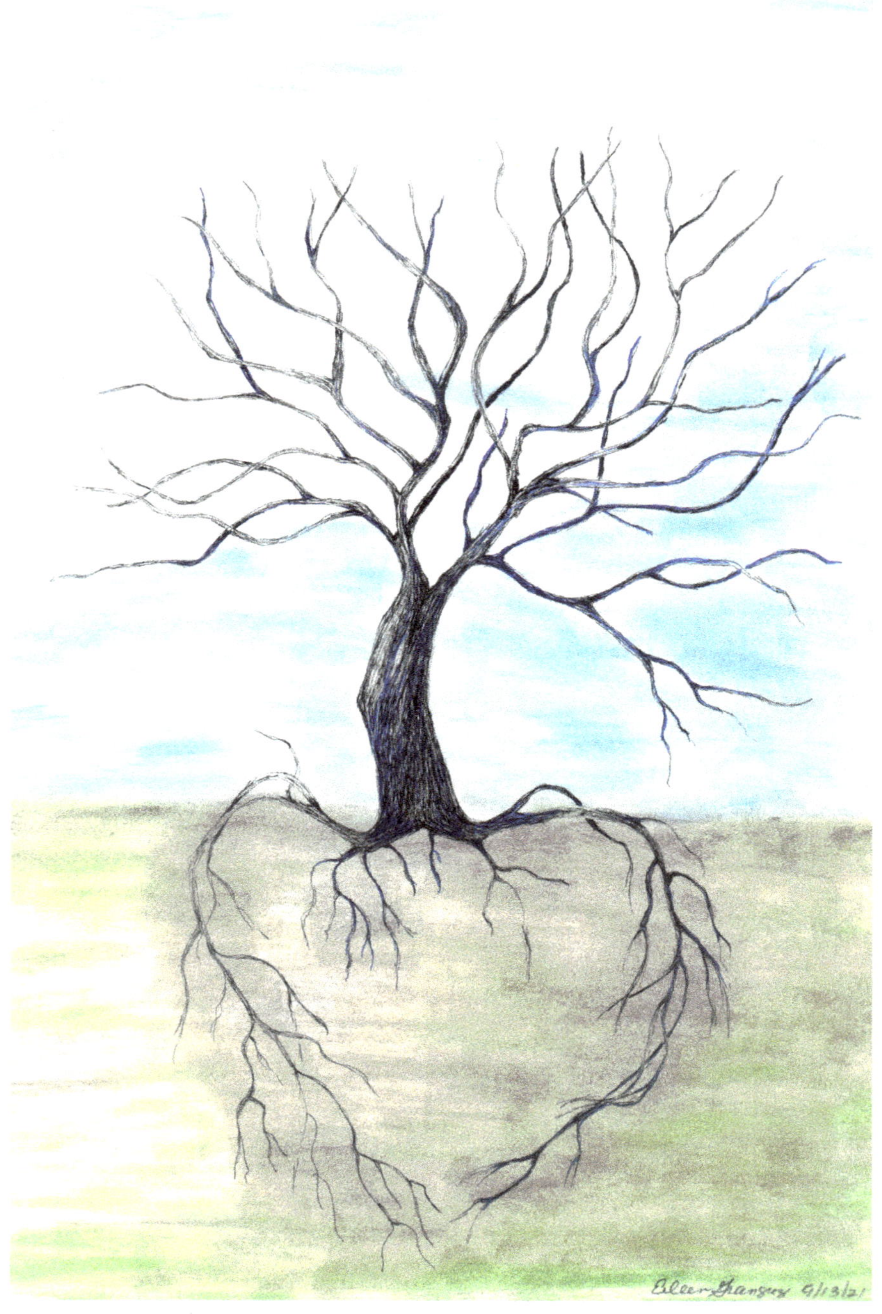
9/13/21

To My Family

To my four brothers:
Acceptance, willingness, forgiveness & humility

To my two sisters:
Serenity & strength

To my mother: my spirit
To her brother: my sobriety

And to my husband: my love
To my in-laws: my all

To my nieces & nephews: my fun
And to my friends: my brothers and sisters.

And last, but not least
To my father, my angel,

May he rest in peace
Forever,

Born, died & always
Remembered in December.

Holly's Lullaby

Welcome, Holly, to God's good green earth!
May your baby blue eyes stay as dear as they were
The night you reached out to me and thought I was Mom.
May you always have everything you ever could want.

So tell me, Holly, how do we survive?
How do we keep from being eaten alive?
Do you know, Holly, the answer to this,
How to keep clear of the dismal abyss?

Yes, Holly, the answer is Love!
The Love that is found by looking above
And underneath and around and at everything,
But mostly, Holly, by looking within!

So when God's good green earth starts to fade shades of brown,
And the sun in your heart starts to slowly go down,
Be aware of escapes that may make you weep,
And remember the three magic words: God, Love, Sleep!

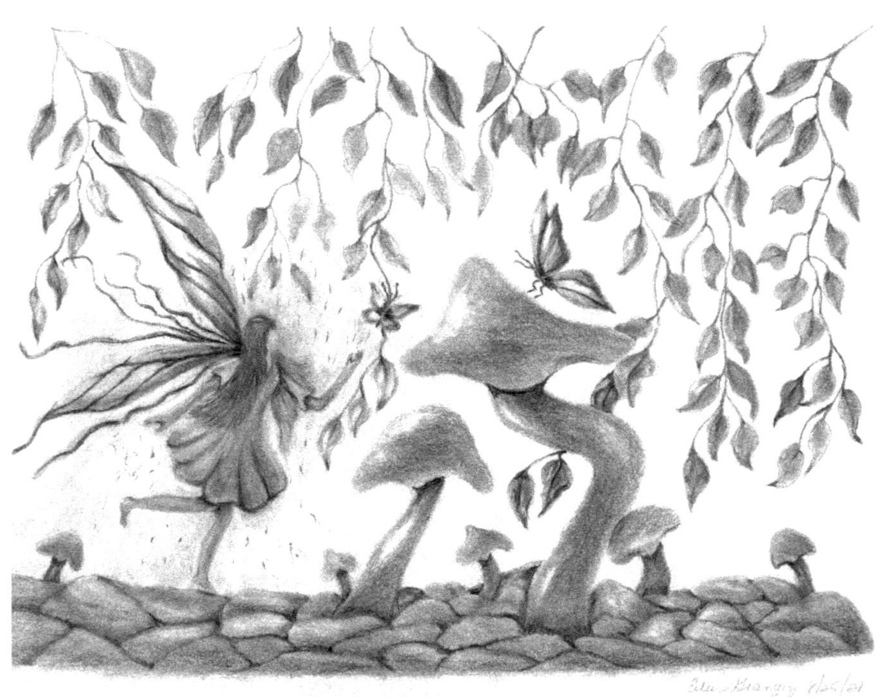

Chapter Three

Whimsy

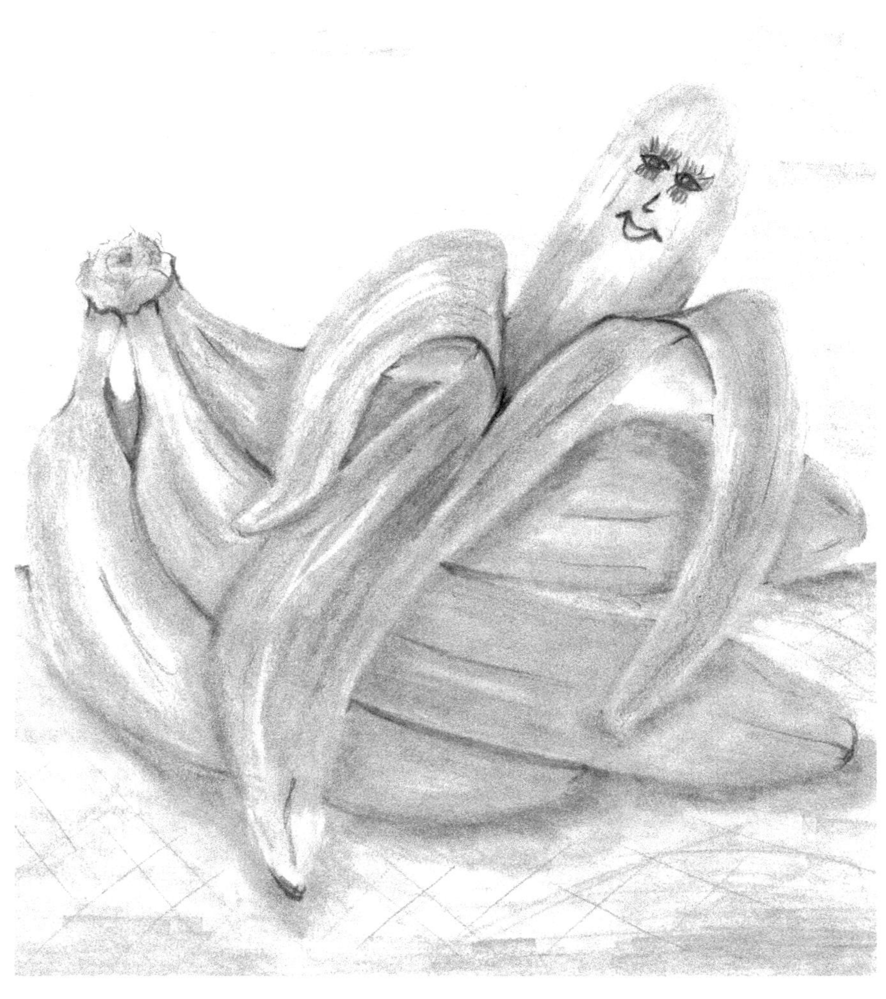

Bananas

In search of the perfect banana,
I go into Ralph's;
He opens the door for me,
I'm hungry.

I look,
I touch,
I smell,
I feel,

I palpate.
It's a good day;
I see lots
of yellow.

Big yellow smiles
lying in wait
offering themselves up
to those who would take.

Bananas (Continued)

Am I good enough
for your mouth?
Am I too firm?
Soft enough?

Am I too green?
Have you ever been
bruised?
You're a throwback.

Then I see them,
this nice, friendly bunch,
every one in their prime.
It's time.

Make a decision,
take me home,
peel me,
naked.

But be careful not
to slip on my skin,
you may not like
the fit you're in.

Ah, but the taste,
the consistency,
the nourishment.
I found it!

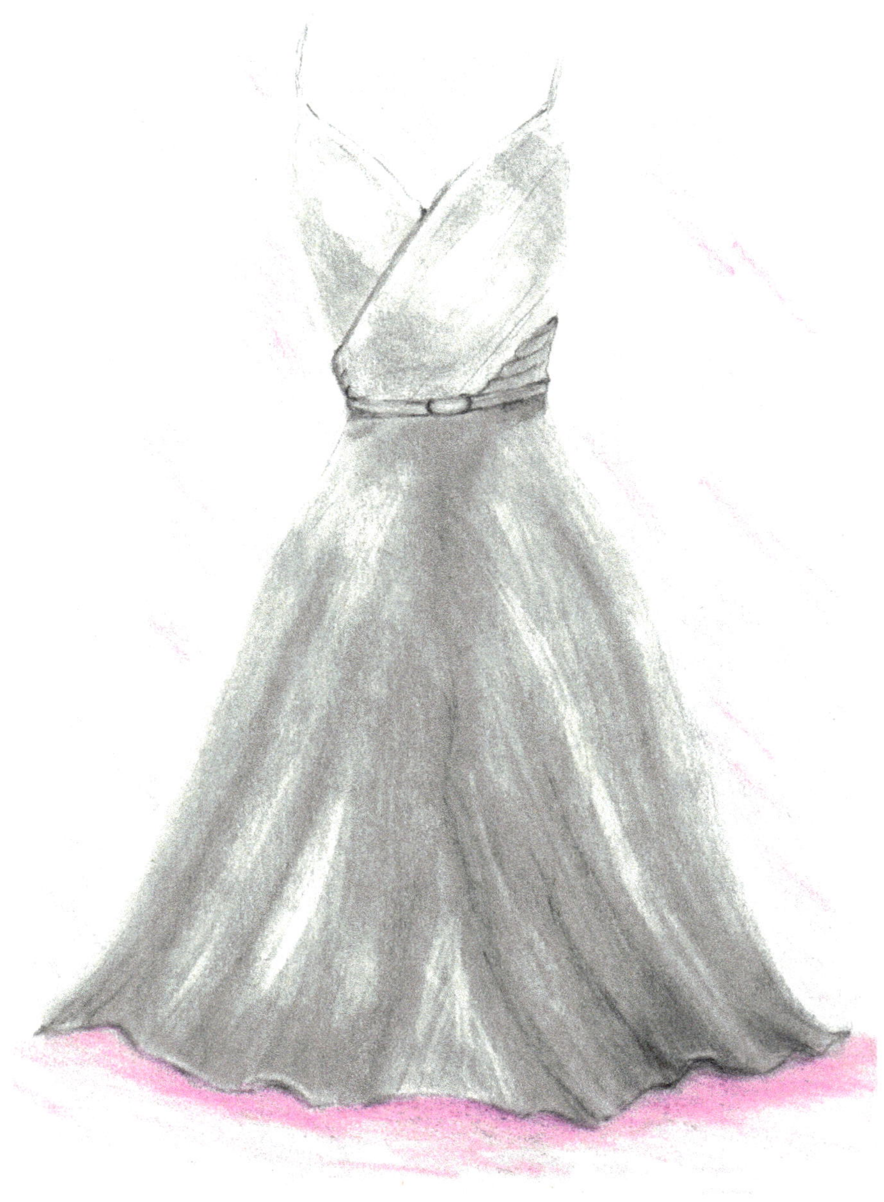

The Dress

I am obsessed
with a dress
and cannot rest
while in this mess.

I must confess
that this dress
is the best
in the west.

But here's the test:
You see, this dress
is in no way le**$$**
than the rest.

And so I guess
that this dress
and my chest
will not enmesh!

A Wedding Poem

Her wedding dress
sings confidence
The wedding ring
Holds everything

Their wedding band
Is on his hand
The wedding day
A sweet display

A wedding vow
Honesty now
The wedding cake
A confection bake

The wedding dance
Extravagance
The wedding night
Two hearts delight

A wedding gown
Of great renown
The wedding ceremony
Traditional yet tony

My wedding wish:
Follow your bliss!

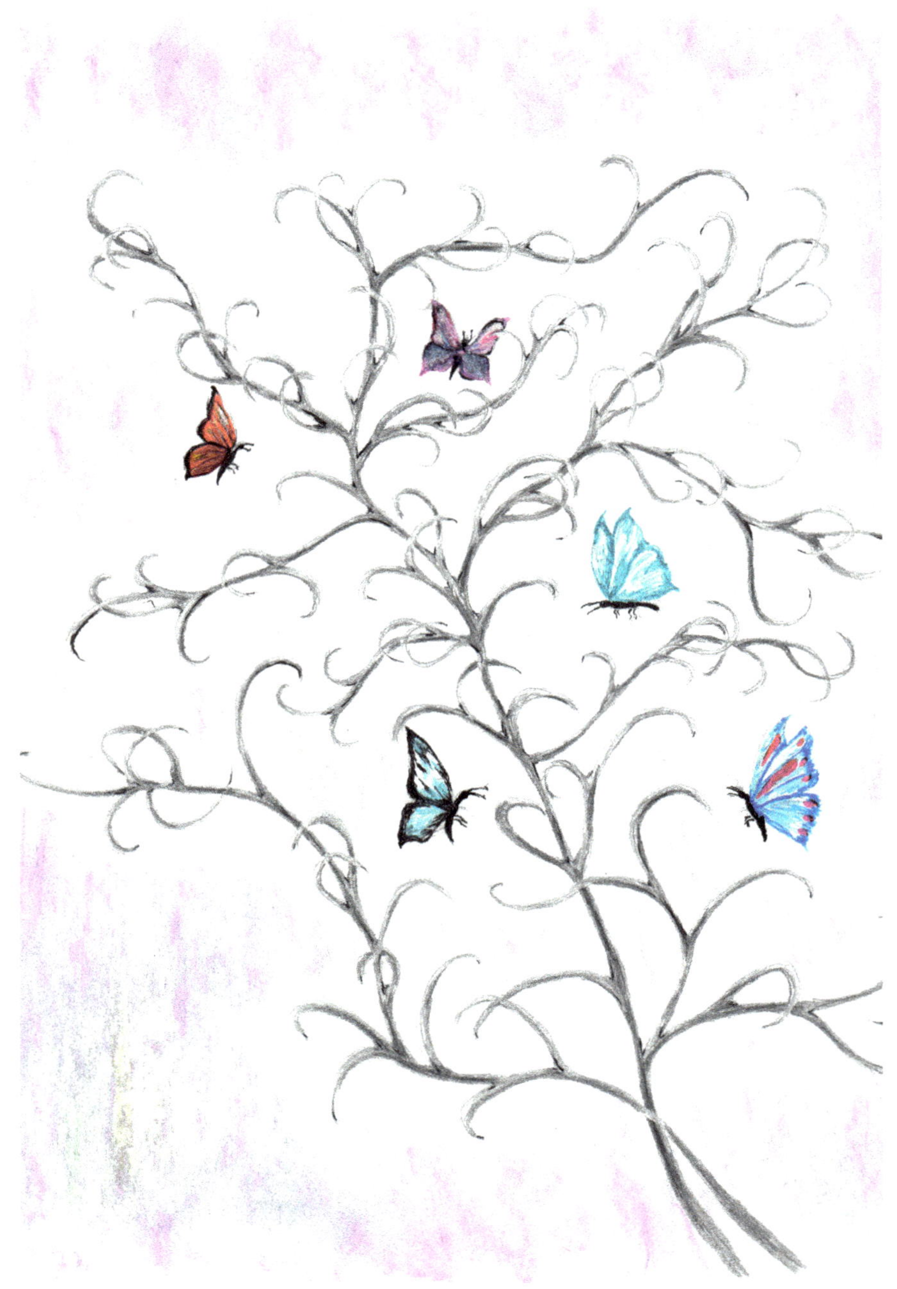

What I Did On My Summer Vacation

What I did on my 40th
Summer vacation:

The hike from hell
Up into heaven
From the desert floor
To the San Jacinto Peak.

Butterflies boldly blaze
A beautiful trail
Then welcome us
To the top.

I thank God

Trees struck dead from lightning
Spiral skyward
To the sky world
Whence their deathblow came

What I Did On My Summer Vacation

(Continued)

I found myself wanting to name
My first born son Alpine
Or Sierra, if a daughter

May the peace of the wilderness
Always be with you

Sweet Summer

Hobo going to Chicago
Lollygagging at Lollapalooza
Riding the rails again
Butterflies having a Green Day

Vagabond daughter
Nobody's child
Big Sister
Baby brother

Honey's sweet
Sporty peppers
Hot dogs
Wonderful weather

Dragonflies dancing
Through the fireworks
Bad romancing
Pyrotechnics

Fun

How much fun
Can I shove
Into one
Old man's life?

Fro-yo for din-din
Vacay in Mandalay
Timeshare in Bellaire
T.V., you and me

Walk in the park
Love in the dark
Wake each new day
Take home the pay

Put it away
For a rainy day
Who is to say
It's not today?

July

Classics all

Baseball

10K run

Summer sun

Years ago,

The last 17,

July the Fourth

In Laguna Beach

When I was young

My summer fun

Was Michigan,

The lake & sun

July birthdays

Rick's and mine

I love your face

That's a nice line

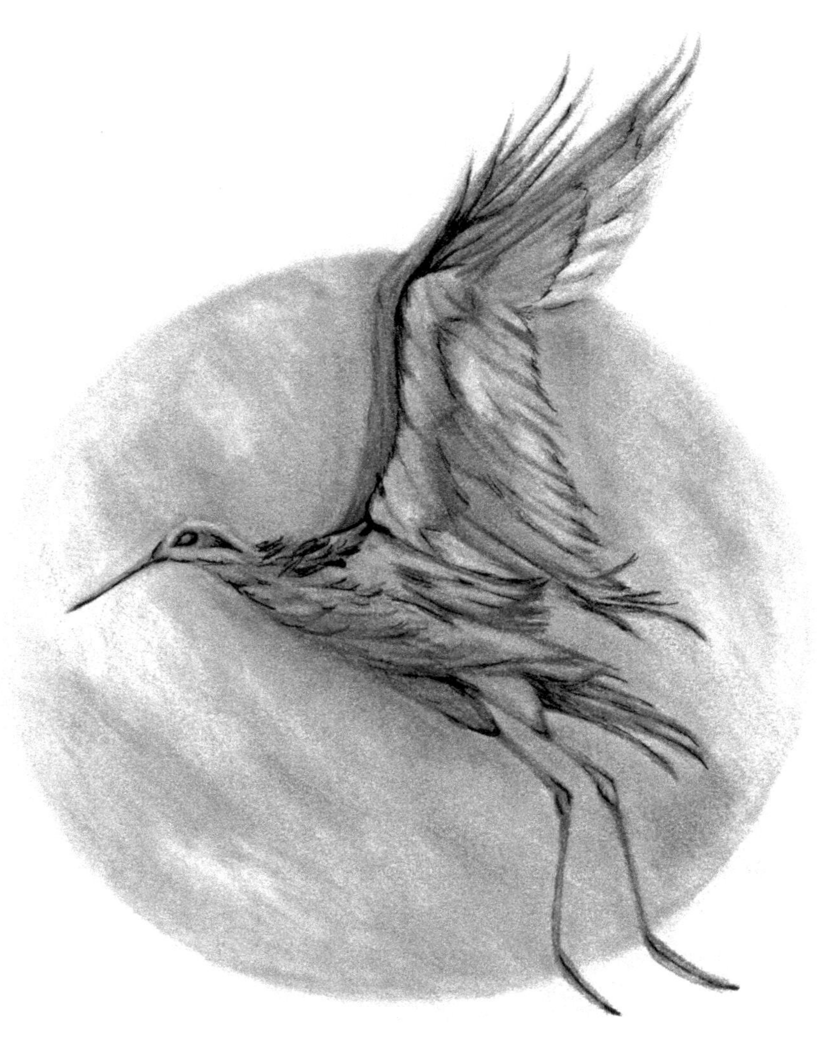

I Go Away

Wanderlust
End of August
No frills, no fuss
Go away, I must.

A women's retreat
Will be so sweet
We'll beat the heat
At 6,000 feet.

Awful
Grateful
Thankful
Hopeful

So go away
I must.
Please excuse
My dust.

Choices

In this great universe,
He is hers.
Ever since they were kids,
She's been his.

Curls and eyes,
Kisses and smiles
For miles of long
Summer days on end.

Choose your love
Love your choice
Until then
Rejoice!

Good wishes are what matter most,
Not what's in your cup.
So choose what makes you happiest!!
Let's drink, and bottom's up!!!

They/Their

Dallas Sun Herwood
Was an hermaphrodite
With a cat
Named Herman.

Their days were spent nursing
Plants and animals
Back to health
& themselves again.

Their nights were spent writing
And reading,
Or going to meetings
Of HA

That's Hermaphrodites
Anonymous
Meetings where they tell us
What it means to be androgynous.

Afterword

I once sent a transcript COD,
Which means collect Cash On Delivery.
Dallas Sun Herwood
Is how my name was misunderstood
And addressed on the envelope returned to me!

Brass Band

Brass Band
Is a caftan
My mom wore
Circa 1984

Golden orange
Dripping with coins
A little bit loud
She looked so proud

Back in the day
My mom would say
C'est la vie
To calm me

Wearing Brass Band
She was the woman
I wanted to be
Beautiful & brassy!

Spectacular Serenity

The other day
I got a ring,
It is the most
Spectacular thing!

I've never been
So full of Love,
It fits my hand
Just like a glove!

To get this gift
Is sheer delight,
Now when I go
To sleep at night…

…I dream sweet dreams
Of joy and peace,
All my concerns
Seem to decrease.

I Love Winter

Wintertime
Is a friend of mine
The cold season
December 22 to March 21
In the northern hemisphere,
Or old age

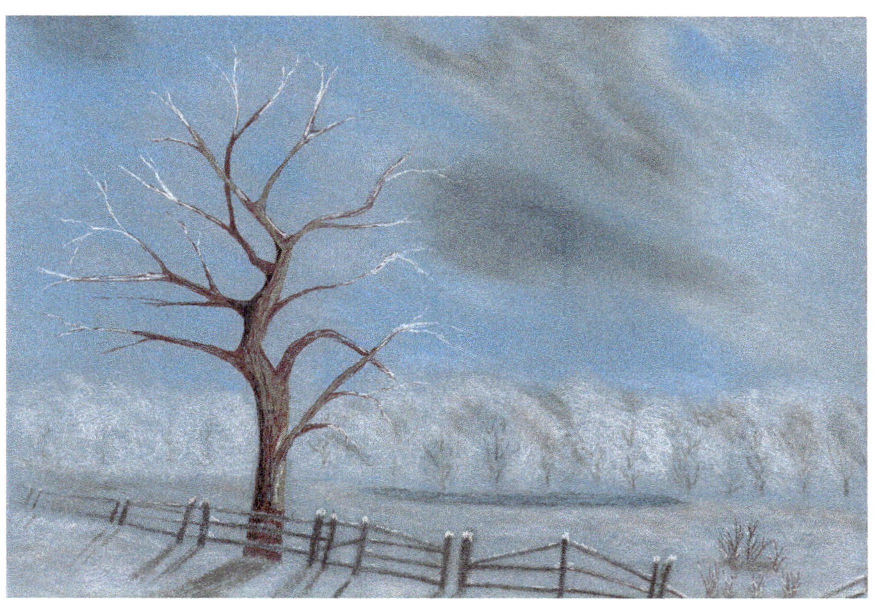

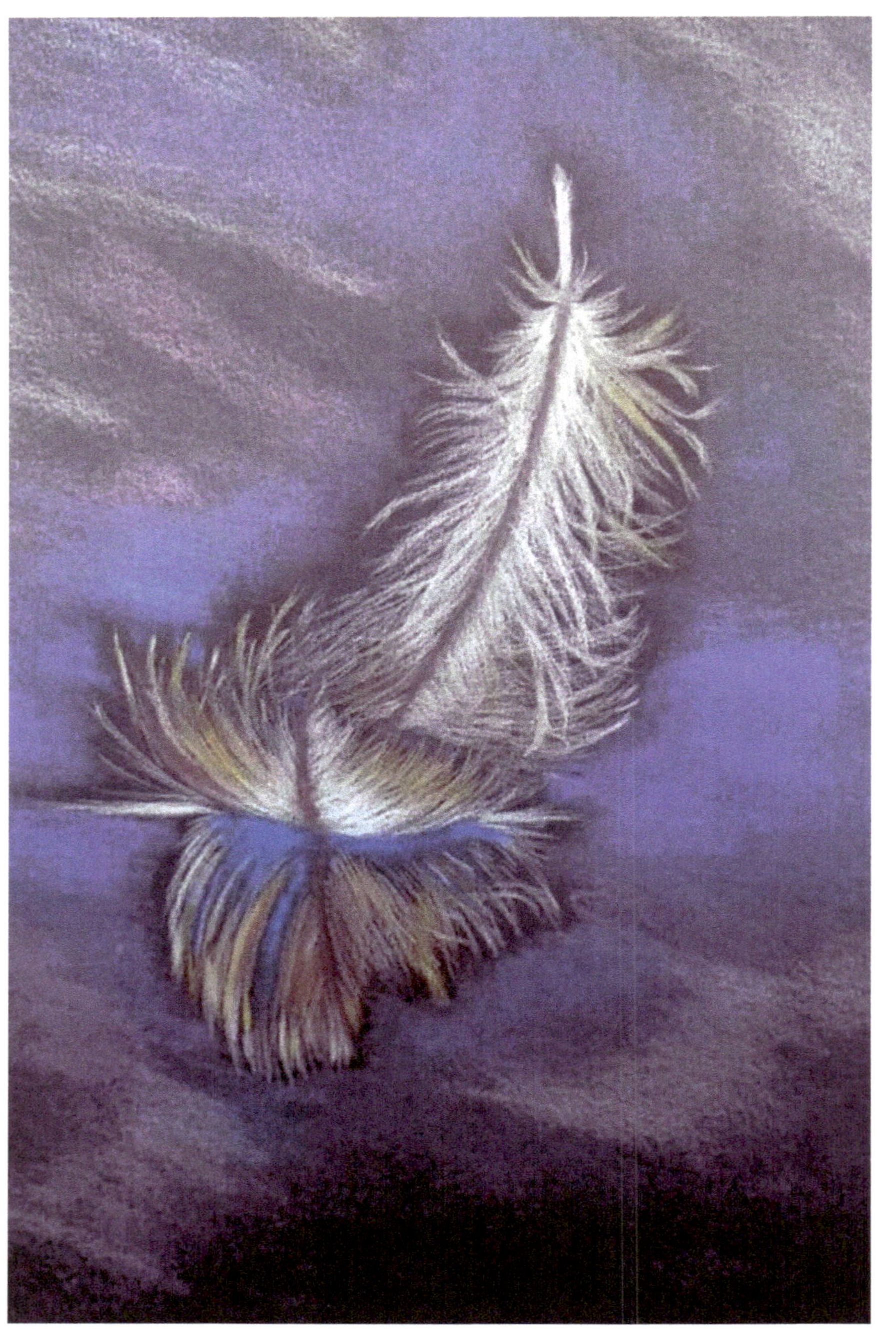

Chapter Four

Reflections

The Philanderer

The philanderer,
He's a wanderer,
Picking up, putting down,
Always running around.

I loved that man,
Such a handsome face,
What an exciting chase,
But we lost the race.

Now our lives are separate,
Tho the memories I'll never forget.
I'll always wish him well,
And our secrets I'll never tell.

All over cuz drugs and alcohol
Wouldn't let us break down the wall.
But I'm free now and feeling good
Just like He always said I would.

My Will

My will of late's been hiding,
My time I've been a'biding.
I'm waiting for what will be,
For what will happen to me.

My mood has been appalling,
The child in me's calling.
What goes around comes around.
I once was lost but now I'm found.

I know just who you are.
My will may take me far,
Or bring me to my knees,
Right where I need to be.

I bequeath you joy and peace,
May spirits never cease
To channel through my pen,
To bring me home again.

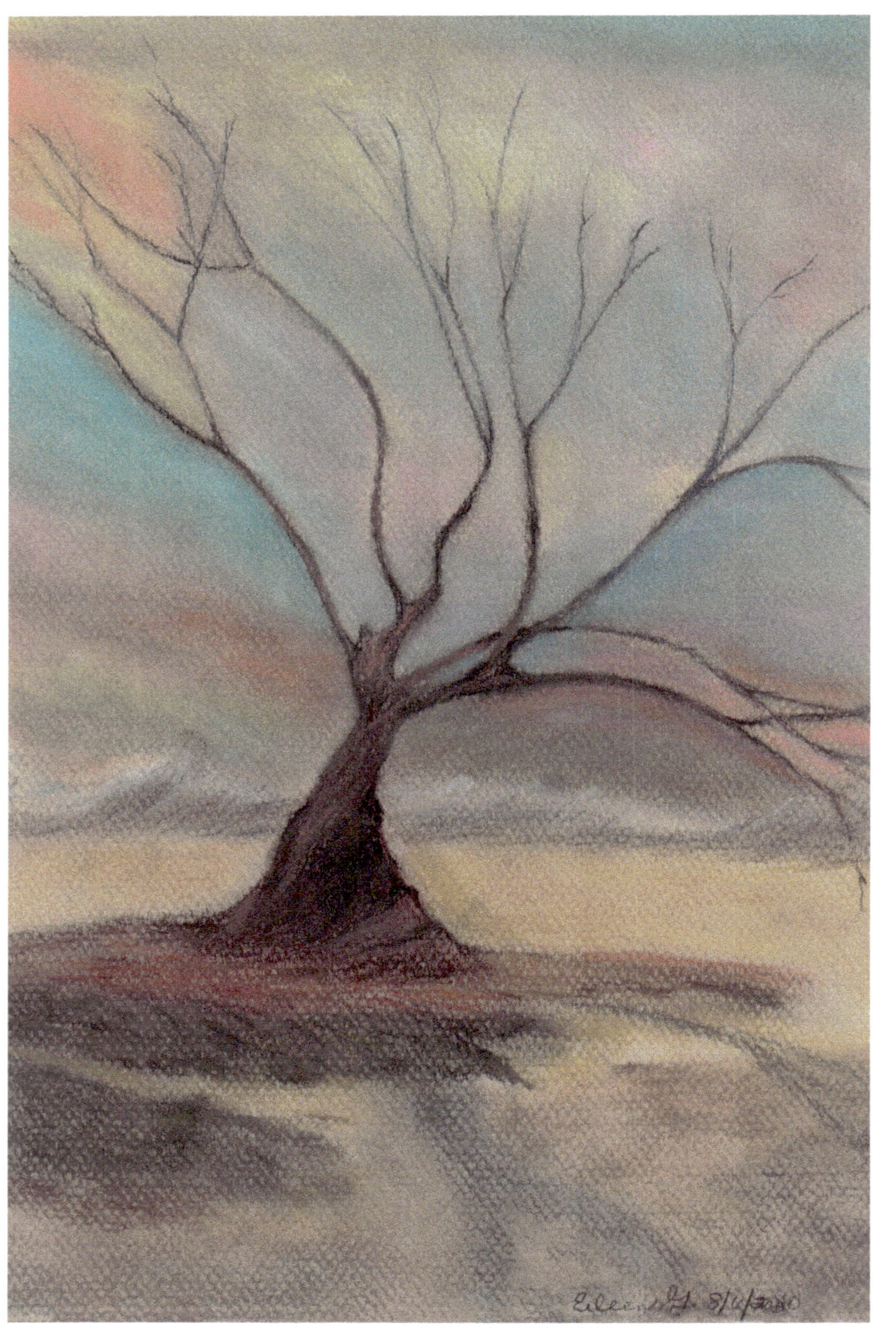

Paradox Blues

God either is
Or he isn't.
Jesus died on the cross
Or he didn't.

Everything is black
Or it's white,
Whether it is wrong
Or it's right.

Serenity will come
And it will go.
Relationships will ebb
And they will flow.

Knowing you
Love me today
Makes that old
Pain go away.

Come

Come crucify
Me,
Little boys,
Little girls,

So that I
May receive
All the sins
Of your worlds,

So that you
May come
Into me
And be free,

So that I
May come
Into you
And just be.

Wet Metaphors

Wet dreams
Drown my sorrows.
Spill your guts, but
Don't put a damper on it.

Drink in the sunlight
Till you're drunk with delight.
Drink from the sea of life
& get all misty-eyed!

Sip from a strong straw
Liquid courage.
Wash your brain
Rinse it clean.

Love! Rain on me
A social lubricant.
A river runs through it,
So pour your heart into it!

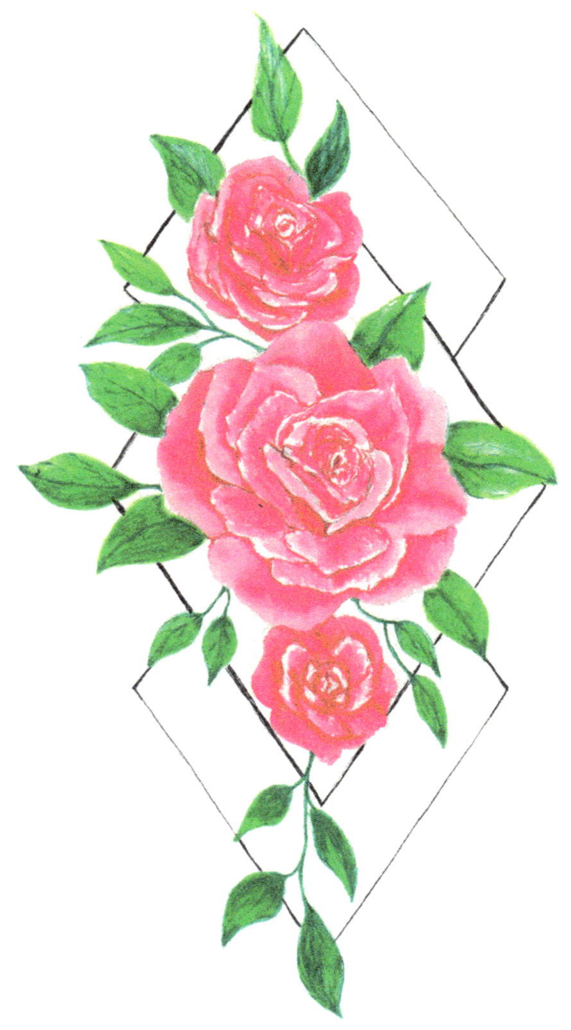

Mother's Day Prayer

Out with the old
In with the new
Out with the one
In with the two

Out with depression
In with the joy
Out with the sad girl
In with the happy boy

Life is so short
Do not sit and wait
Come on people
Let's cohabitate

Out with alone
In with together
Just one more month
And I'll be feeling better

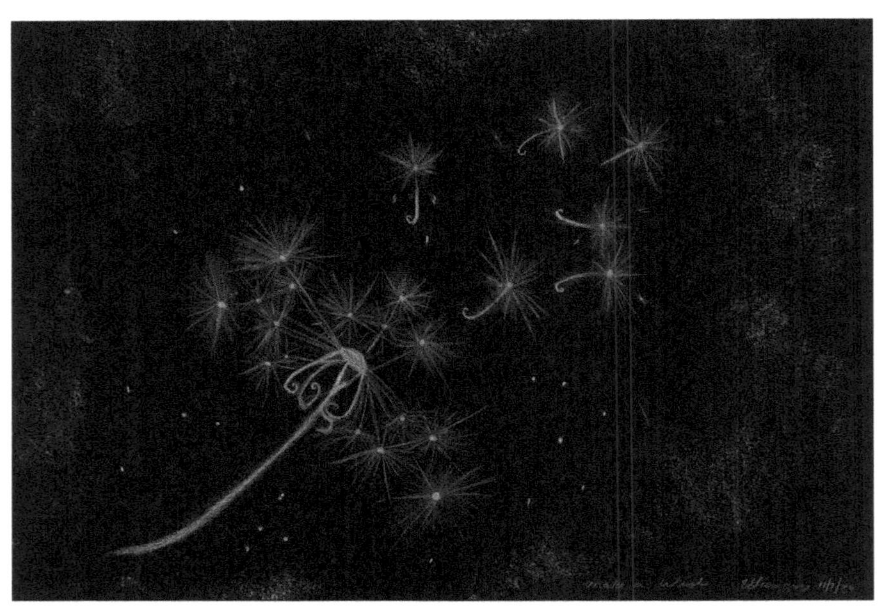

Change + Challenge = Life

I went to a conference
For a couple of days
I conferred so much
And in so many ways

It was a first for me
Yet I felt so at home
With friends and family
Yet I felt so alone

I love my work
I love what we do
I miss the old times
But I relish what's new

For a girl from the sticks
I've come pretty far
When once I did wish
Upon the first star.

Summer Of Freedom

Where are you when you feel most free?
Anywhere on a beach
Meeting friends for coffee
In a hot air balloon over the Serengeti.

What does sweet liberty mean to me?
Being at home with family
Cuddling up with a very good read
Rediscovering the Coachella Valley.

When I see freedom, what do I see?
Someone completely out of custody,
The island chain of Hawaii
The smiles of Louie and Melody.

Mind your head, free your mind
Let go of faith in all mankind
Love your voice, voice your love
Encourage others to rise above.

My White Privilege

My white privilege
Comes from the knowledge
That both of my parents
Were Yankee northerners

Who drove their family
Across the country
Via Route 66
The chute down which

Everything loose
In the good ol' U.S.
Fell into
Southern California

Thank God
There are laws
And courthouses
In California

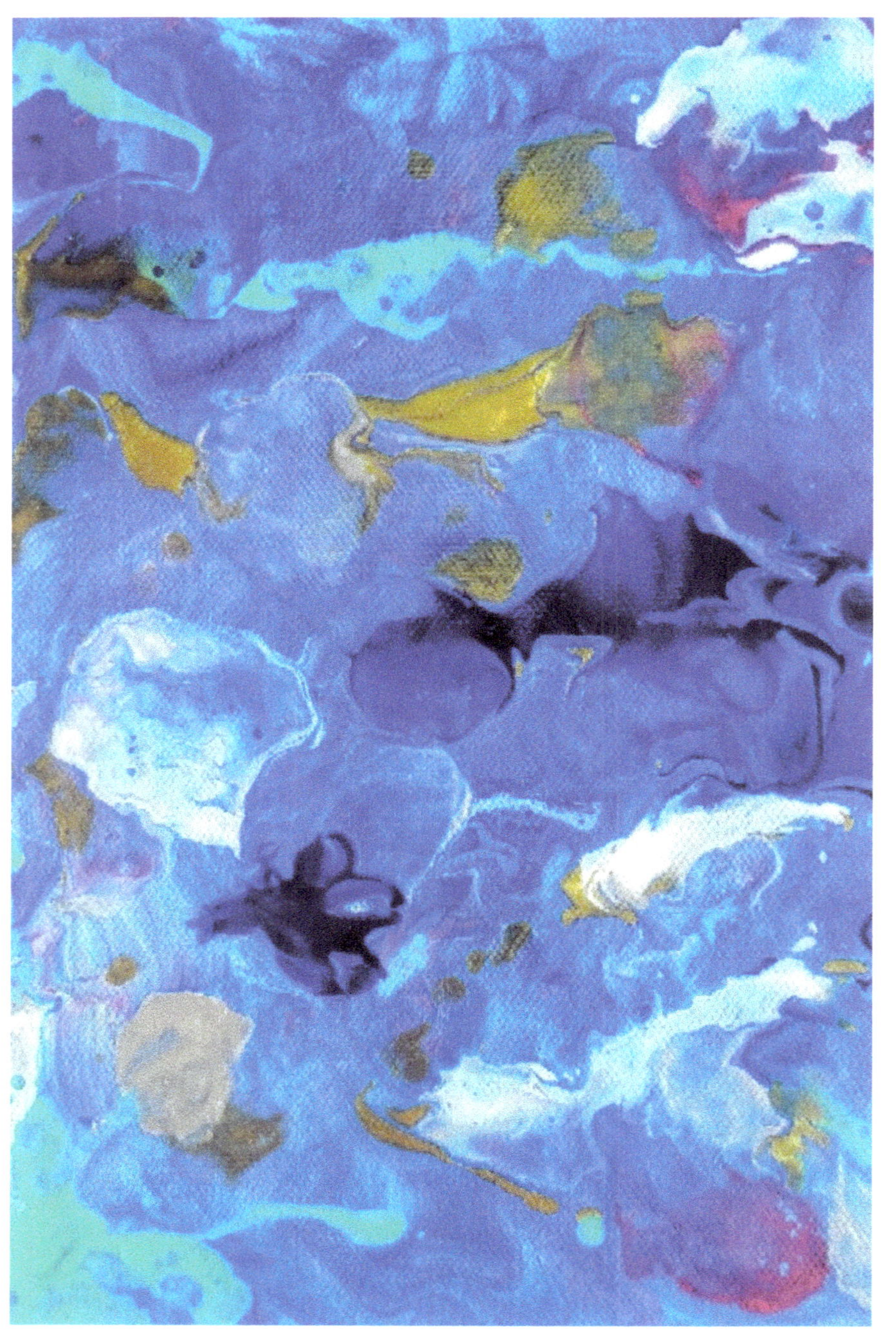

Why Is It?

Why is it that poetry
always sounds better
when you're blue?

When you're happy
and you write it,
it sounds like you're a fool.

I guess sometimes
you're feeling
too romantic,

And other times
you're feeling
frightfully frantic.

But whenever
you're feeling
all's right with the world,

Why Is It? (Continued)

You never
seem to write it
'cause you're a happy girl!

Shadow Dance

I laid my Corona beach towel d
o
w
n

I finally realized my dad was g
o
n
e

It's all a matter of the here and n
o
w

One thing's for certain: Life goes o
n

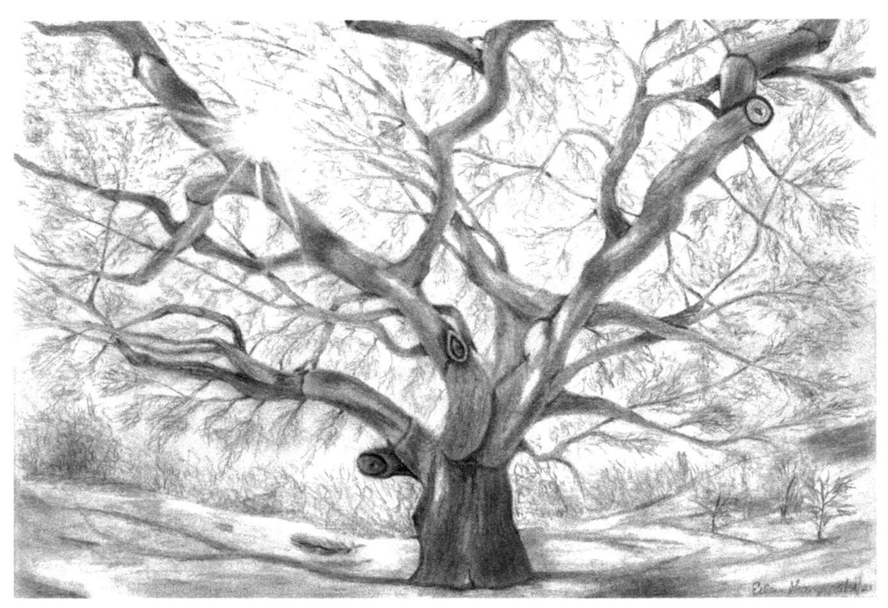

What's Life?

"What's life to you?" I ask you now,
the what's, the when's, the why's, the how?
You say, "Survival," with simplicity.
I say, "Life's more than that to me."

It's ups and downs, highs and lows,
how long it lasts, God only knows.
But I'll take the challenge willingly
to see what God has in store for me.

He says there'll be people along the way
who'll steal your heart and soul away,
and when you plead for what's rightfully yours,
they'll turn you away and slam the doors.

But on sunnier days when you're with me
and we're hiking up towards the oldest tree,
life's sweet as candy, beautiful as flowers,
and if we choose for the taking, life is ours.

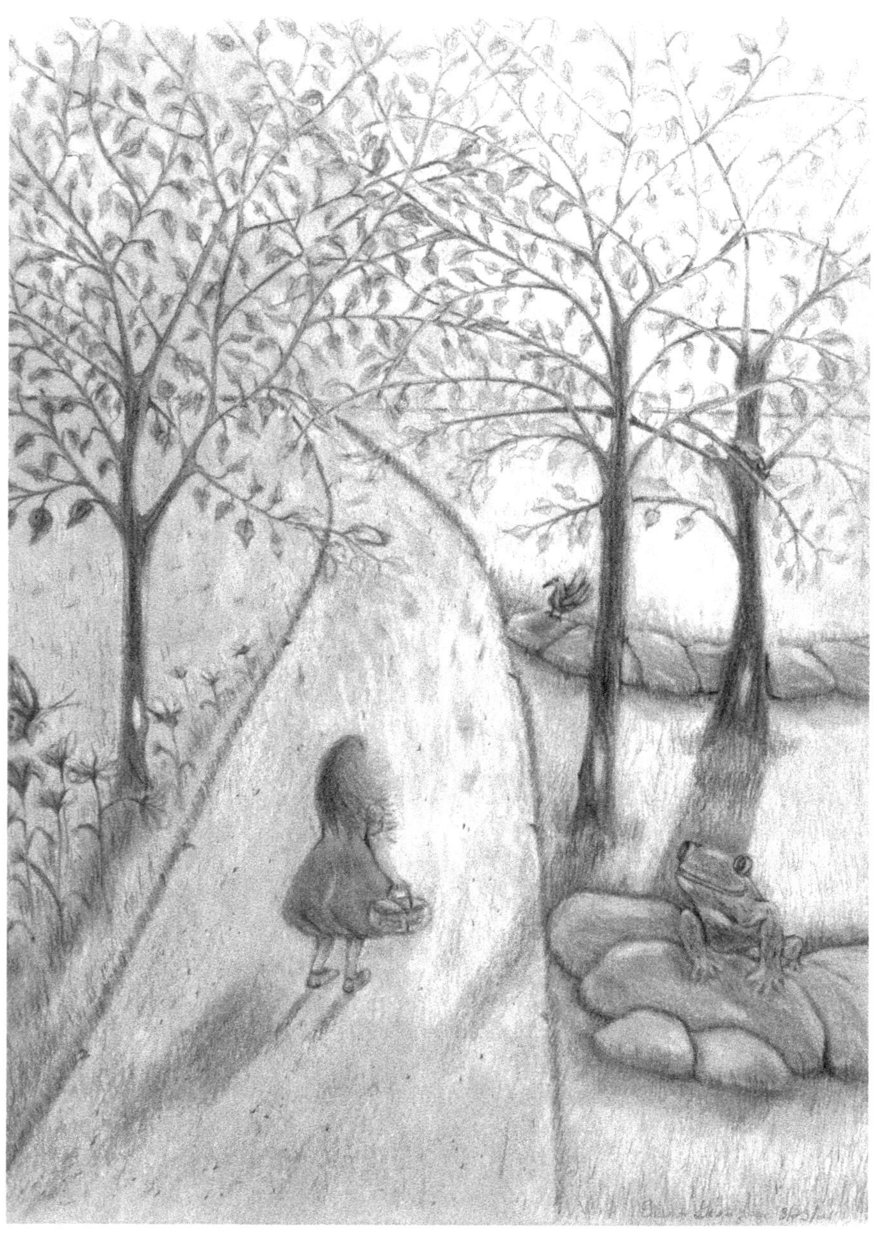

Chapter Five

Contemplations

I Love You

I tried to love dishonesty,
I tried to love fear,
I tried to love my father,
But he was never here.

I held tight to the pain
In the dark of the night
Till I finally let go
Of my futile fright.

I listened for the answer
And sure enough it came.
God is the answer
And Love is your name.

I love you each day,
Each fresh, new beginning
Keep caring and sharing
And grinning and winning.

Adolescence

Adolescents,
Seems their essence
Is to fuck it up
And disrupt

Every generation's
Imagination
Must come forth,
Of course

I recollect
What a little shit
I may or may not have been
At ten

A word to the unwise
Open your eyes
Wear sunblock
& we're here, if you need to talk

Gratitude

Running water
Being my parents' daughter
Each dawn's early light
My eyesight

My fingers and my toes
My ears and my nose
Friends like you
My husband's true blue

Learning to read
Teaching to seed
Food to eat
My hands and my feet

My family
The sky and sea
The help I get
Retirement!!!

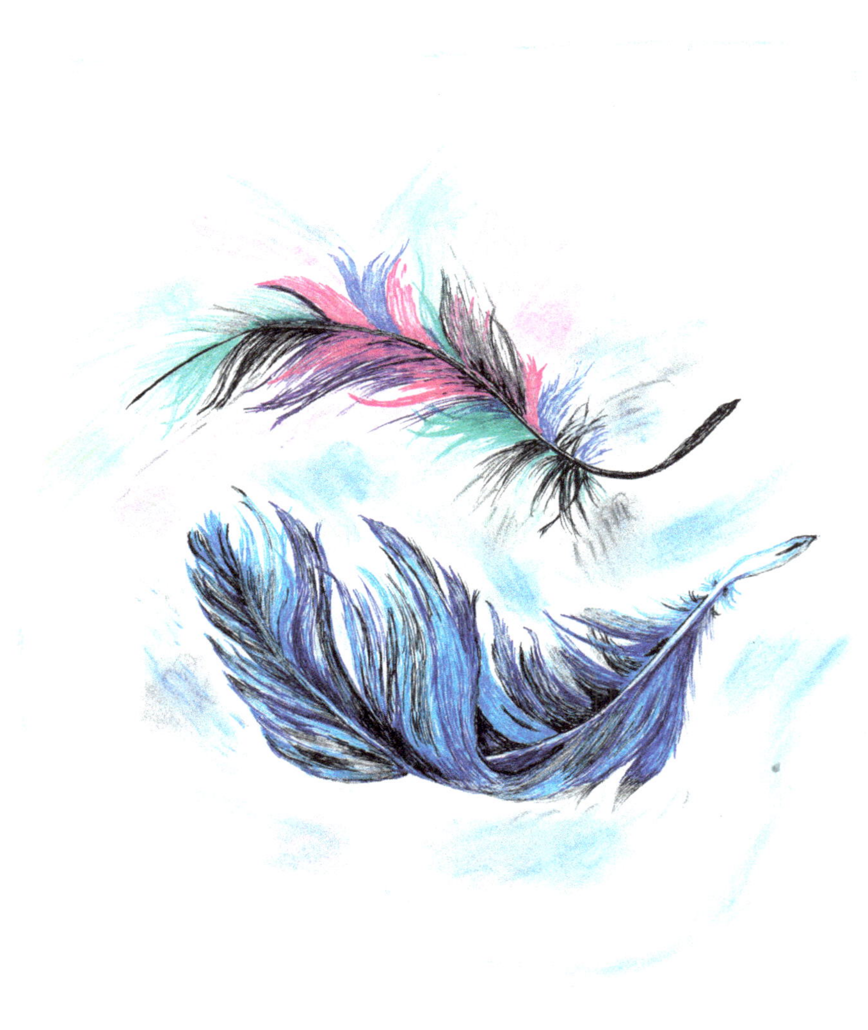

Dear God

Dear God
I am alone
I want to be
Night dreaming

Far away
Sex in bed
Or in my head
What's it all mean?

This crazy scheme
To get ahead
Live right now
I don't know how

I wish I could
Do something good
Worth more than gold,
Than just growing old

Dear God (Continued)

Before my time
Just passing time
Sharing a rhyme
With Father Time

Gang Love

They're good people
They love a lot
They listen in their steeple
They sweat when it's hot.

They live life to the fullest.
They meet death at its door.
They're riddled with bullets.
They cry, "Please, no more!"

They're in the mob.
They're in the desert.
They have a mom.
They have a sister.

Oh, baby,
Sons and daughters,
Strip yourselves
Of those colors!

Time

Time is a tricky mother
It sneaks up on you,
It will tell,
It flies when you're having fun,

It heals all wounds,
It is Father.
You spend it with someone
It is money,

Time is love,
The love of your life.
I had a great love
This time.

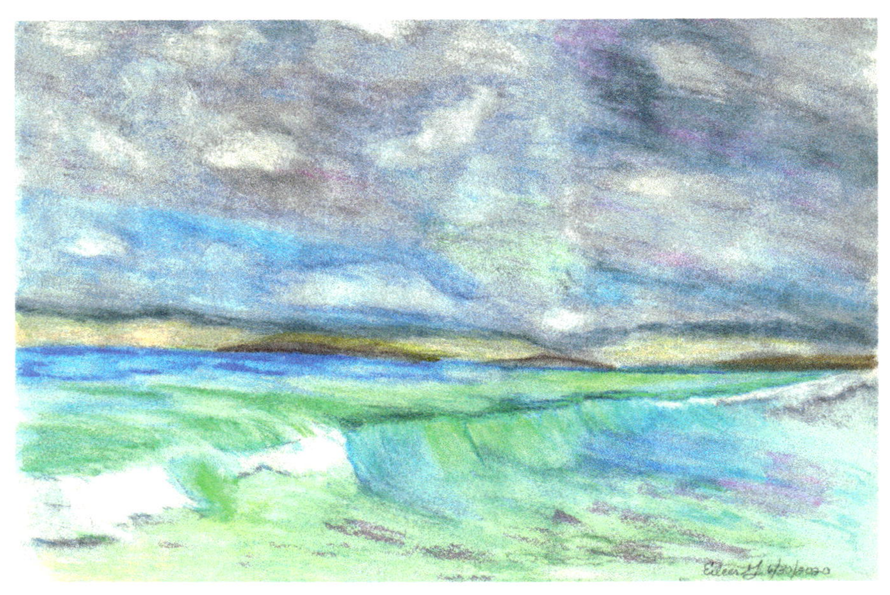

Life Is A Beach

Waves of sorrow,
Waves of joy,
Little girl,
Little boy.

Waves of gratitude,
Waves of grief,
Shifting sands,
Coral reef.

Waves of happiness,
Waves of pain,
Salty foam,
Sweet refrain.

Yes, life's a beach,
And then we die.
Thank you, God.
Why ask why?

My 65th Summer

A silly summer cold
Feels like quicksand in my soul
Aging gracefully is the goal
It's so intense, this getting old

Some rude advice from me
Medicare is not free
It won't cover corrective lenses
Just the doctors' examinations

My fashion sense has changed
"SilverSneakers" is all the rage
Maximum coverage for when I go out
Super skimpy for around the house

I'm into puzzles and my PBS
And sitting at my writing desk
In my purple Puma shower shoes
I've got the 65th summer blues!!!

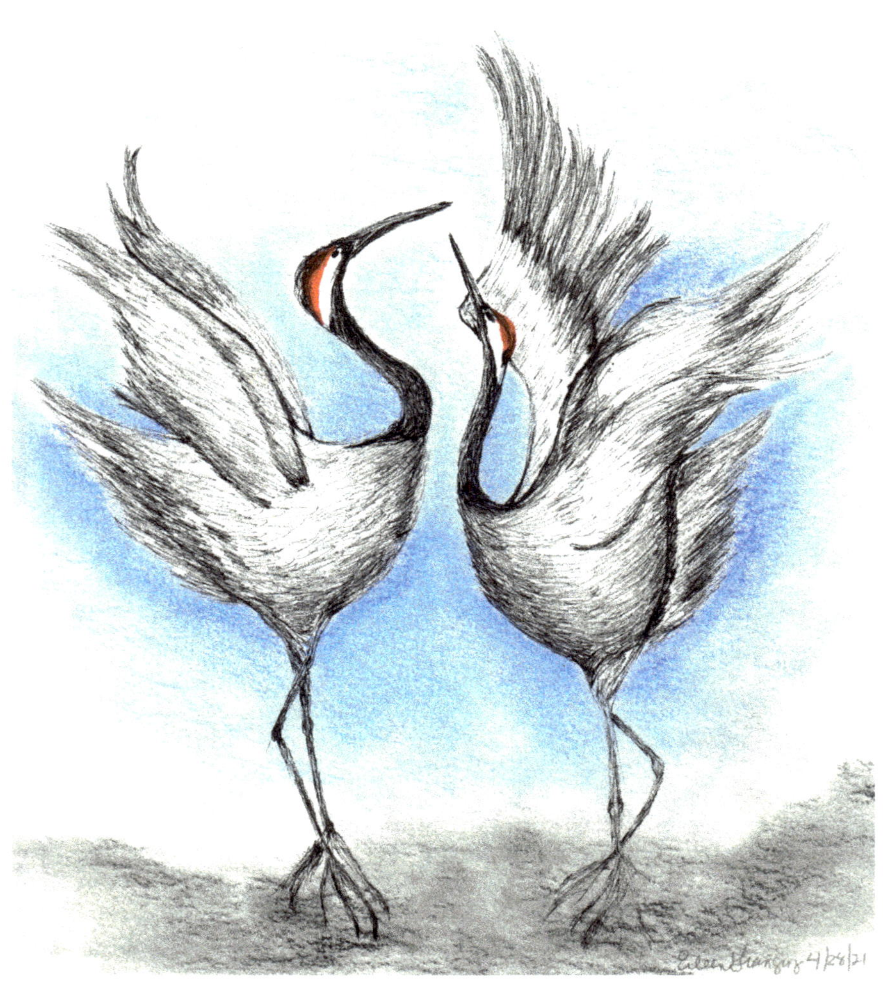

Chapter Six

Friendships

Ode To Lisa

Little, lovely Lisa Shivak
Took a wrong turn, never came back.
Down and out, beat to death,
Coke and pot, booze and meth.

I recall the younger days
Before we fought the purple haze,
Cute young things without a care,
Our biggest worry: what to wear.

Off to see the world were we.
She ended up hung from a tree.
Her murderer had killed before.
To him she was his little whore.

To me she was a sister/friend.
I pray I may see her again.
But for the grace of God go I.
I love you, Lisa. Why'd you die?

Professor Coldheart

Professor Coldheart, Professor Coldheart, put on a sweater!
Life out there will always get better!!
Of course it takes the right attitude,
But that shouldn't be hard for such a good looking dude!!!

There's music and mountains and work that we love,
There's the help that we get from the Man up above.
There's family and friends and food that's fun,
There's golf and softball and swimming in the sun.

We wish you success in your new-found job.
Excuse me a second while I choke down a sob.
May you make lots of money and meet lots of girls,
The two most important things in the world!

Come back and see us when you need a vacation
Or maybe for an upcoming special occasion.
I can assure you that you will be sorely missed,
Just try not to make your new boss so pissed!

Giving

Dear Caroline,
It's a state of mind
What can I do
To be of service to you?

Friends giving,
Thanksgiving,
It's a way of living
& it's never ending.

How can I help?
It starts with yourself.
Making the world a better place
With a smile on your face.

Dear Caroline,
You are a friend of mine.
I have always loved you.
Giving thanks for all you do!

Toni's Treasure

Here's to Toni's baby,
A precious baby girl
May she have heaven's health
And all the wealth of the world

May she have her mother's eyes
And her father's disposition
And her mother's creativity
And her brother's inhibition.

May she inherit her grandmother's
Perseverance
And greet life's brooding
Interference...

...with smiling eyes
And a happy heart.
May You sculpt her life
As a work of art!

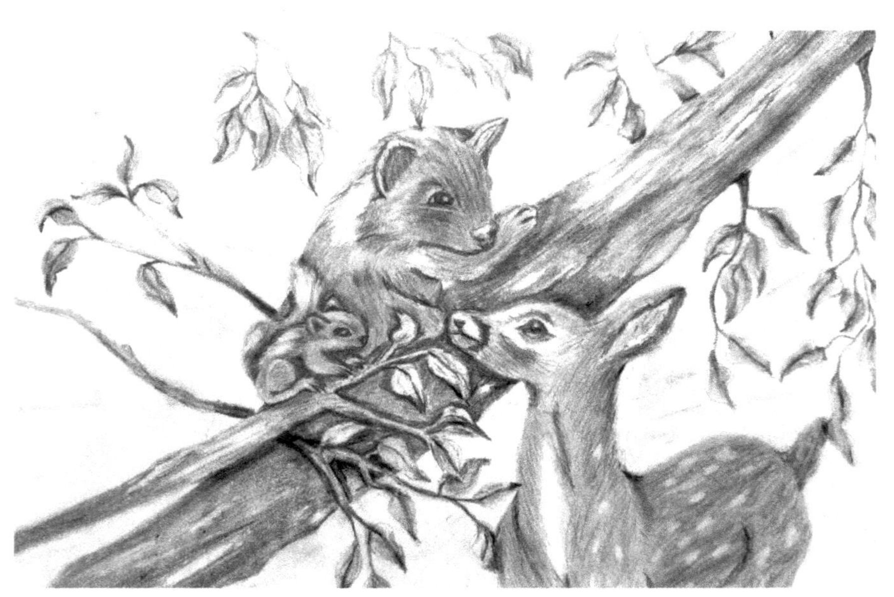

A Small Circle Of Friends

Friends of Dallas Ann:

Georgeann

Cheryl Ann

Royann

Dolores La Vera

Eileen

Jan

Lisa

Louise

Beth Ellen

The rest

Shall remain

Unnamed

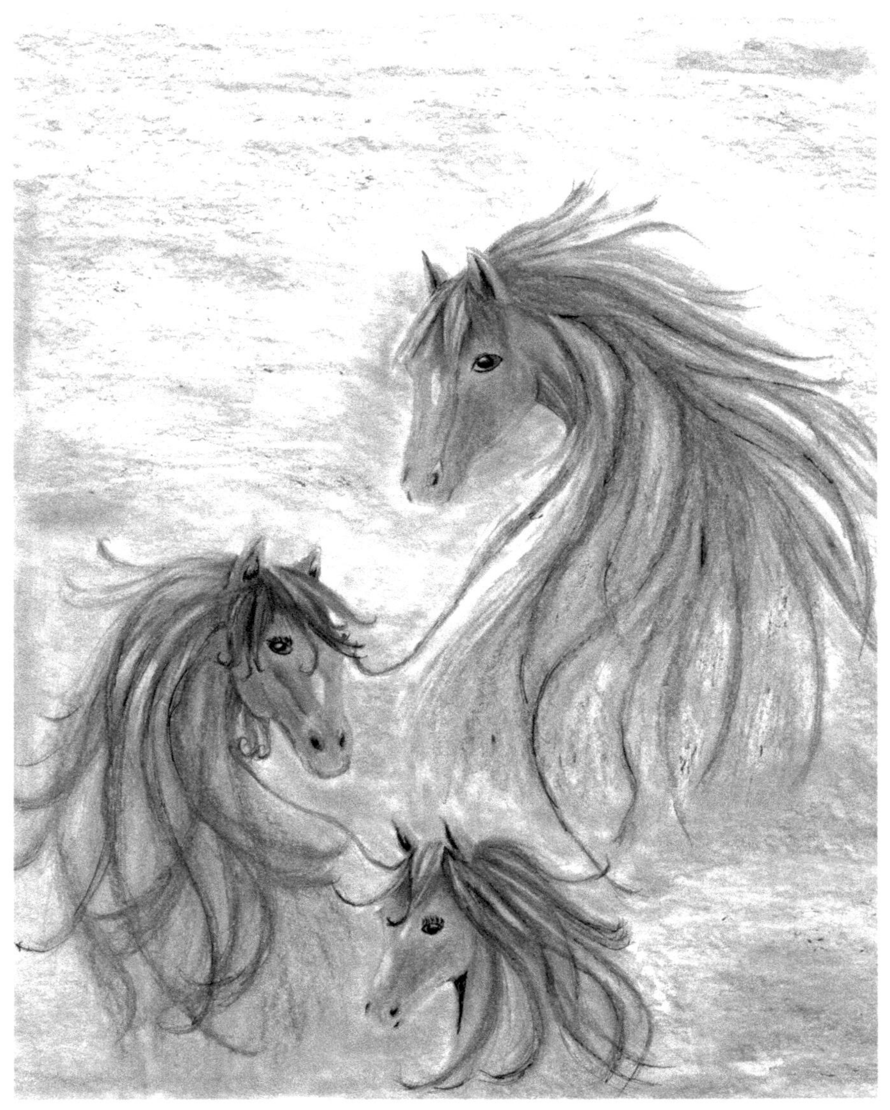

Magic, Toni And Me

She's deep and dark and she has no secrets
She lives in a mansion behind a tall fence
Her name is Toni, but she's really Magic
Creativity and love flow whenever her eyes blink.

I remember the day, the first time I met her.
My initial impression was, "Unforgettable!"
A forever-type friend met smack in mid life,
Someone you go to through troubles amid strife.

We hunted for horses in her Mustang convertible.
Her opinions and ideas are incontrovertible.
When we finally found one on which we could agree,
We saddled up that appaloosa filly.

What a wonderful ride our friendship has been!
Her miniature pony was even given my name!!
Love and acceptance of each other's our code,
The nicest horseback I ever rode!!!

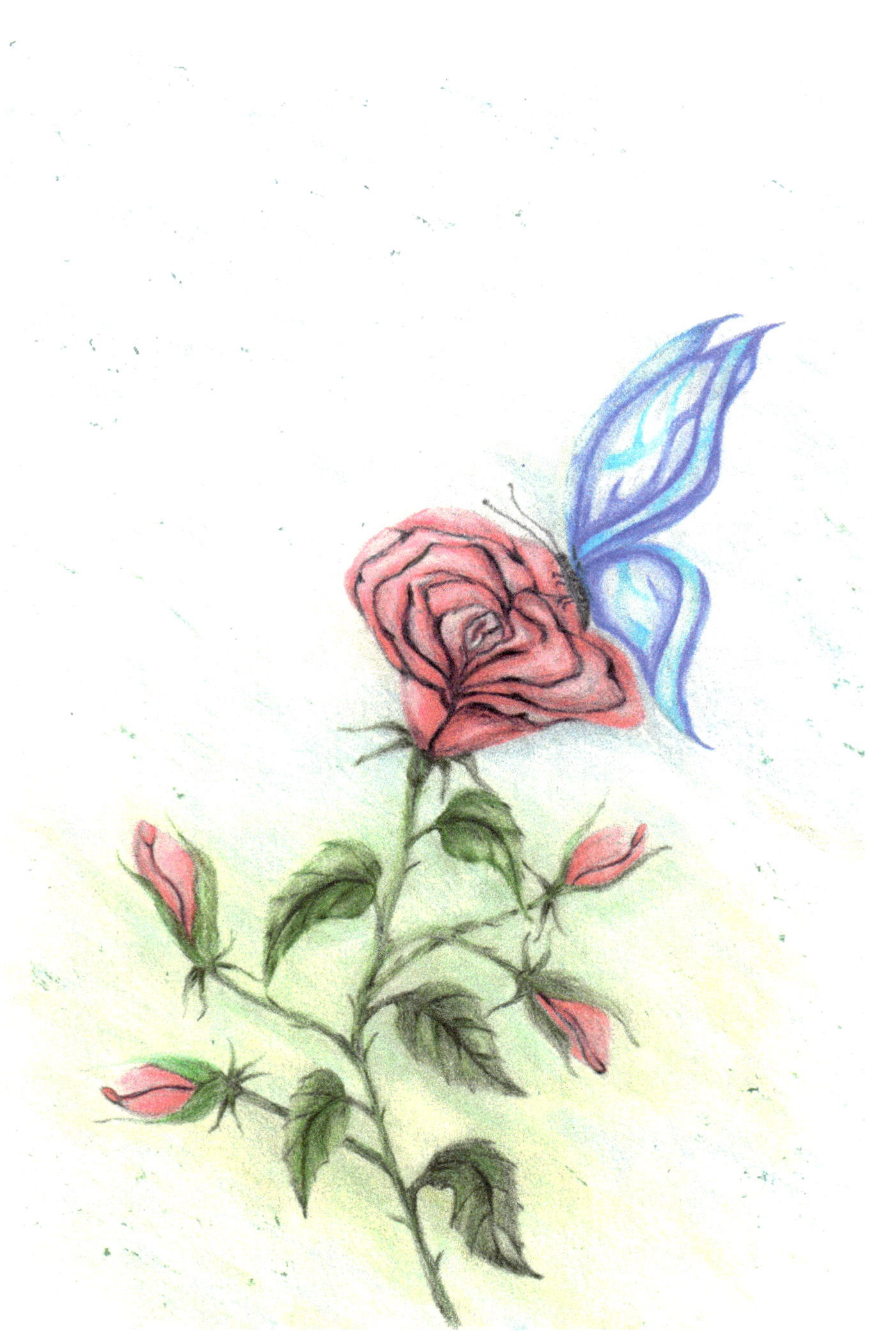

Butterfly Rose

Lonesome Destiny
A little girl's name
Two little sisters
With faces the same

I had a little sister
Whose name is Nicole
She wanted my heart
I gave her my soul

Met my new little sisters
On a mid-January day;
It began with a rainbow
Raindrops on sun's ray

How did we meet?
God only knows
Viviana & Ashley
Butterfly & Rose

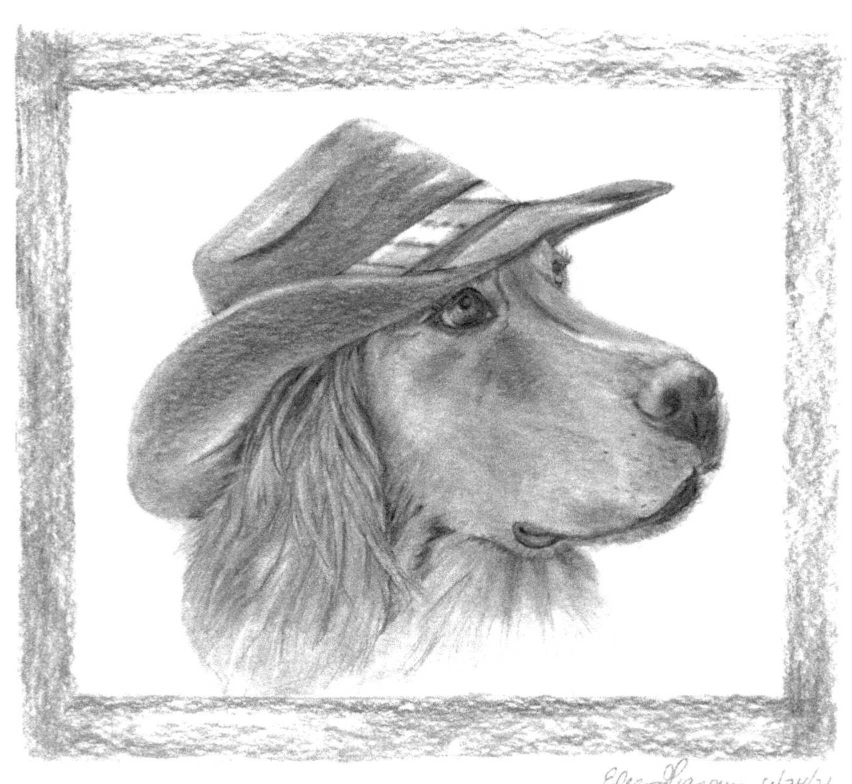

Chapter Seven

Furry Friends

Walking Our Dogs Indy and Valentine

The prowler,
The prancer.
He's a howler,
She's a dancer.

He leisurely pees
While she patiently waits.
He's a big tease
She's his first mate.

She went white
Completely overnight
When we brought him home,
Our pouncing puppy boy.

Our Funny Valentine,
Independence Day Dog
Both named
For the holidays they came.

Belong In The Zoo?

I belong in the zoo.
How about you?
Guinea foul squawking
Sweet smack talking

Klipspringer springing
Beckoning spring in
Here comes the rhino
Taking full control

Families come running
to let the sun in
on their day,
on their way!

Shellie the giraffe
had her baby calf
143 pounds, five foot ten
of pure giraffe joy – The End

Zeit Thelma Mistoffelees

Our precious Thelma
A sweet tuxedo cat
Late this morning
Had a heart attack!

2012 - 2021
Nine years,
Nine lives,
But this life won!

I first named her Zeit
After German "time."
We didn't know her gender
And got her on 9-11

So we assumed
She & her sis
To have been "resumed"
The first of August

We named her sister Geist
As she was gray as a ghost
And could hide anywhere in plain sight
She was Zeit's protective host.

We renamed them
Thelma & Louise
After we learned
They were twin sissies

Then I added Mistoffelees
As every cat needs three names
I'll miss her teethy kisses
And her cuddle-on-the-couch games

Yes, she had a sweet life
With her dog & cat sissies
My pink-nose love
Zeit Thelma Mistoffelees

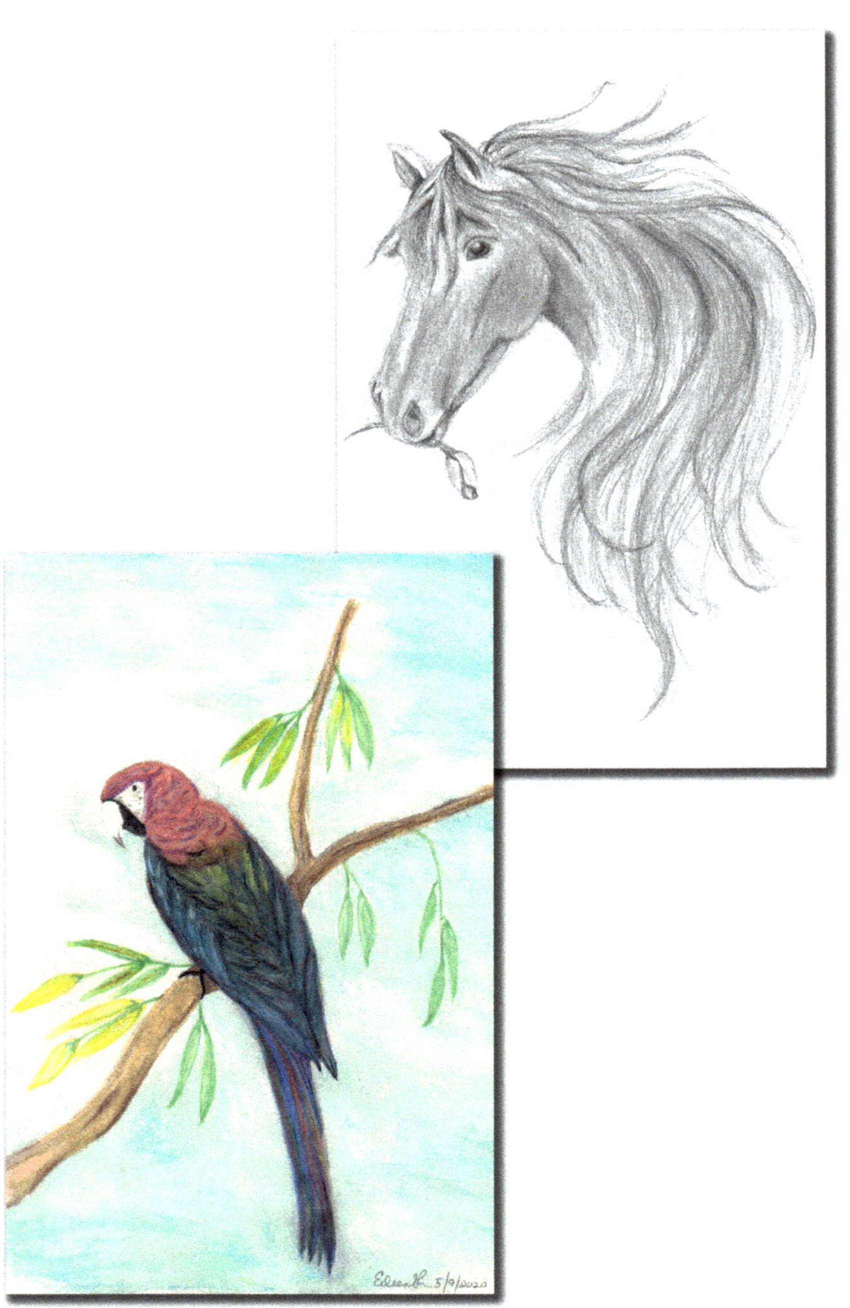

Pets Past & Present

First there was Bad Cat,
white with pretty blue eyes.
Then came Sadie,
a poodle in disguise.

Then Chips of Magic, my horse,
but Sylvester the Cat came first.
Then Ricky's messy bird,
Oliver Wendell "Holmes" was the worst!

Our Funny Valentine,
was man's best friend.
Then Rick got me Harry,
another bird again!

Then a bunch of kitties
with cute kitten names.
We're a big happy family,
& animal lovin is our aim.

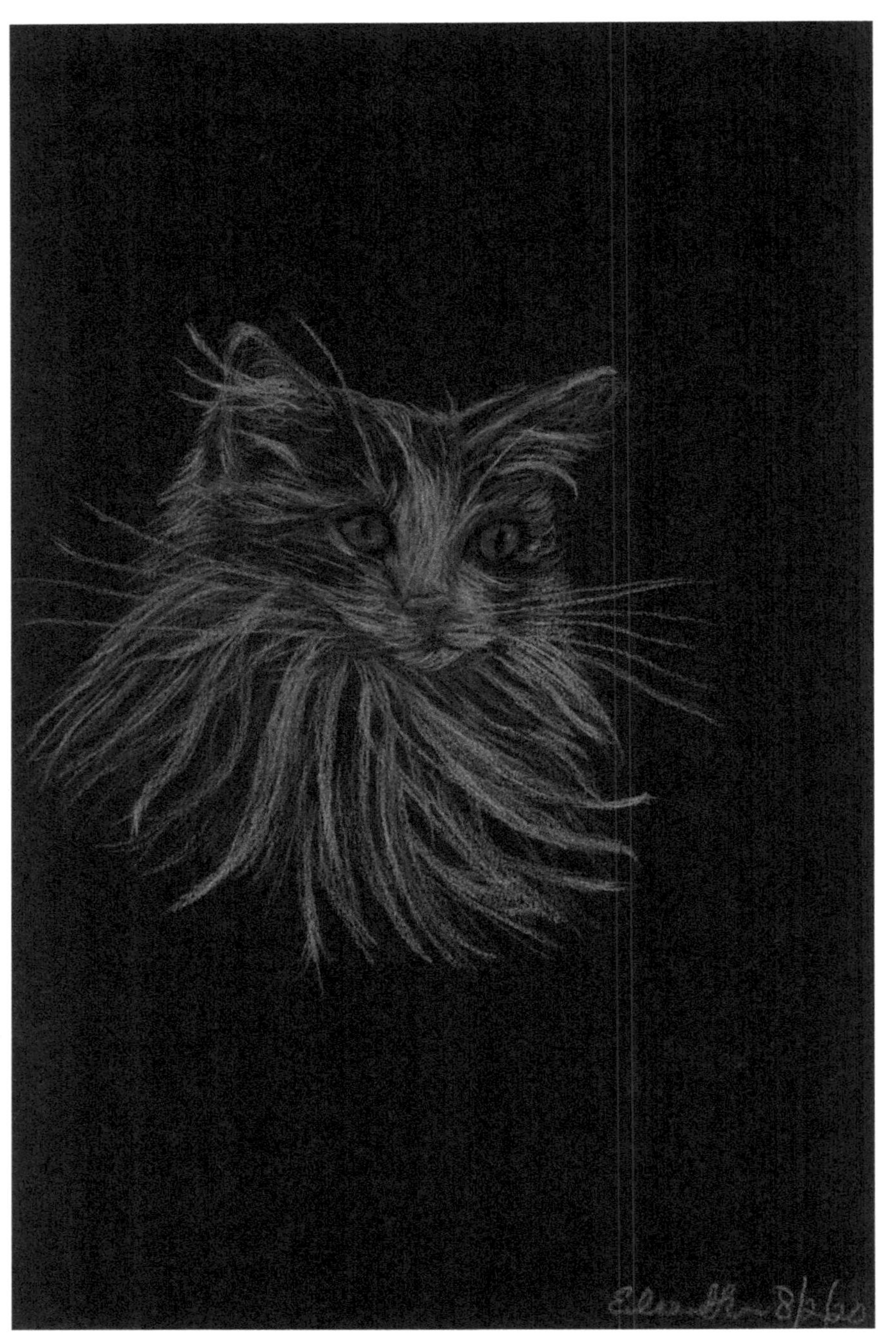

Sly's Eyes

As blue as I felt
The day he died

As hard as it is
To admit I lied

As deep as the sea
As strong, as wide.

I'm touched by his soul
A stalwart guide.

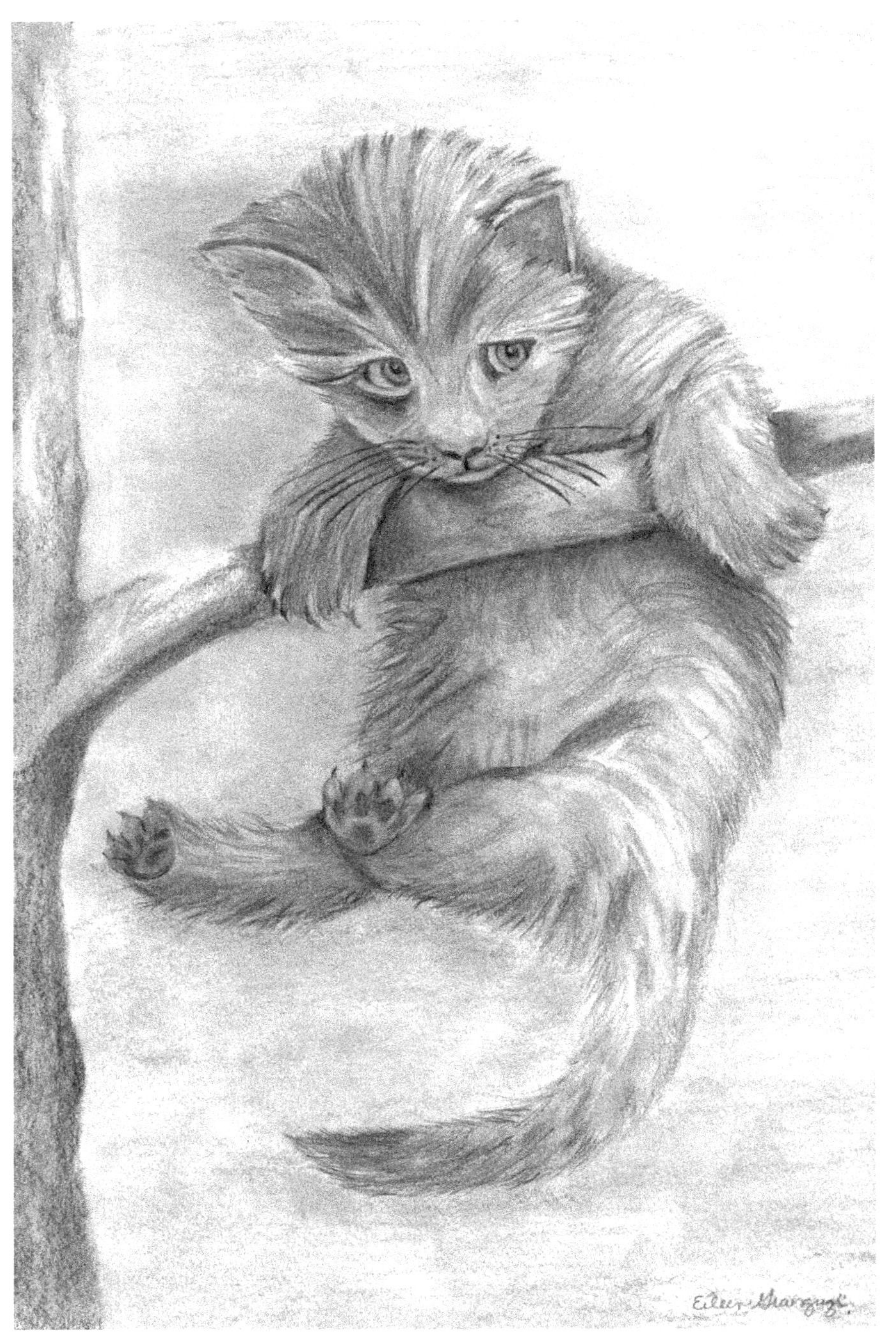

Name The Cat

Angel kitty
Santa claws
Baby face
Pinky paws?

Old Blue Eyes
Baby Frank
Felix the Cat
How about Hanks?

Little Tiger
Cottonball
Yoyo Llama!
Babydoll?

Named the cat
For his dad:
Rudy II
Precious lad.

Sly S. Hinkle

Such a handsome cat,
So furry and fat,
When he purrs with joy.
He's my little boy.

I wonder which life he's on
And what it was like back then.
He's brought me warmth and fun.
My beautiful feline friend.

He keeps me company
In the middle of the night,
And when he wakes hungry,
His belly ready for a bite,

We fight our way to the kitchen
To begin a brand-new day,
I feed my hungry kitten
And go happily on my way.

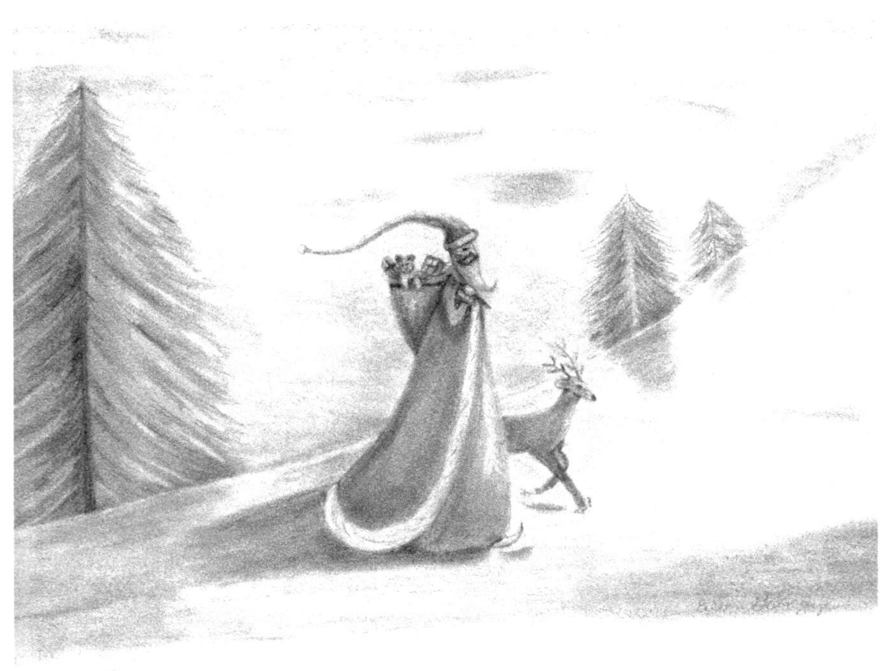

Chapter Eight

Holidays

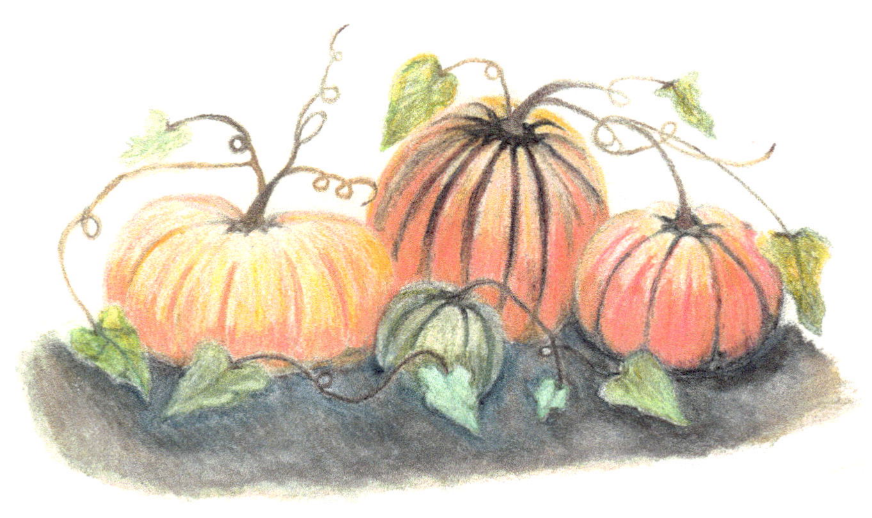

Thanksgiving 2020

I was thinking thankful thoughts
Rainfall just like diamond drops
A fire in our fireplace
Sunlight shining on my face

Winds of spirit, winds of air
Blowing through my heart and hair
Memories of family fun
Golfing in the Santee sun

Being wanted, needed, loved,
Understood, respected, heard.
Angels all around me serving
Thanksgiving dinner nice & nourishing.

Snow-capped mountains up up up
Cats Thelma, Lou & Sari pup,
Even with this physical distance,
Wishing you all a Merry Christmas!

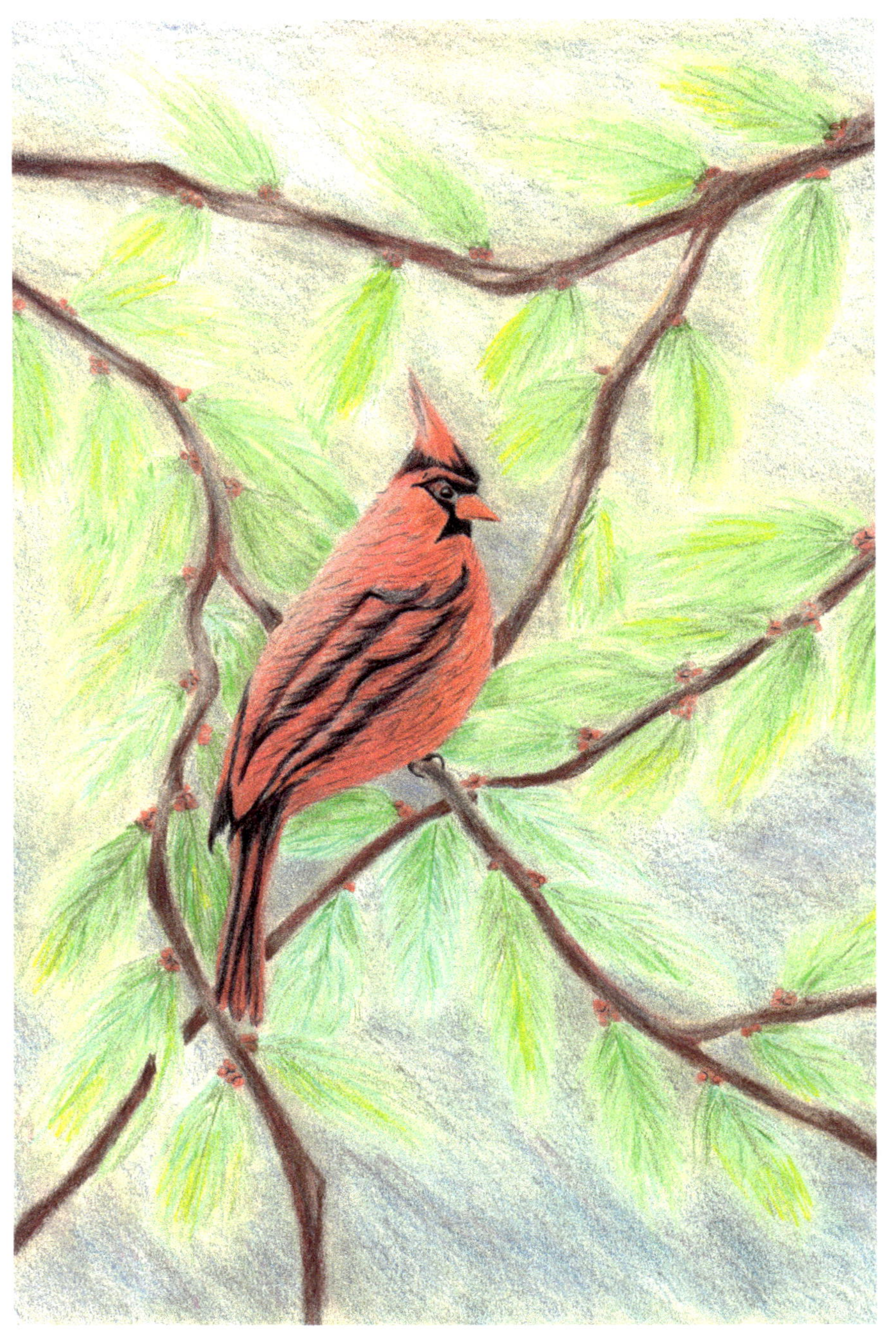

Christmas 1985

Dear Dad, sweet Pop, darling father o' mine,
You'll always be my number one valentine!
Although our relationship could be characterized as distant,
The bond of love between us has been silently consistent.

I've always considered myself my father's daughter,
And my mother, your wife, well, I never quite caught her.
My brothers and sisters are all so exceptional;
You taught us there's more to life than being intellectual.

I've finally found my own sense of balance,
No longer am I perched precariously on that tall fence
Waiting to fall from the slightest whirlwind,
Crashing when I hit bottom, wondering how I had sinned.

I hope this poem doesn't blow you away,
It's the only way to express what I really want to say.
Merry Christmas, Dad, and Happy New Year!
May all your days be happy ones and your years full of cheer!

Happy Earthday

Happy Earth Day
The world's worth day!

Get rid of gas today!!
Put Earth first today!!!

Quit taking our precious
Planet for granted

Or you'll be feeling
Sorrow tomorrow

Skating Free In Santee

One Christmas morn,
All safe and warm,
I woke to find
Black skates of mine

I had such fun.
I'd just begun.
So fast and free
Just being me.

My childhood
Was so damn good!
Now that I'm old,
It shines like gold

Just one more thought,
One of a lot:
Gratitude
Is my very best mood!

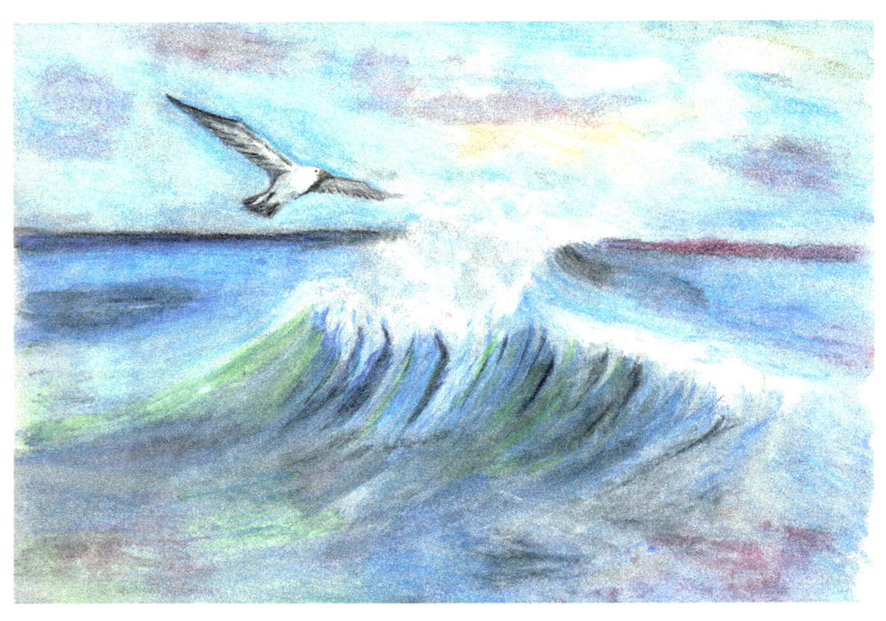

Chapter Nine

Trips

Hi Birthday

Easter at the St. Regis
Was a fashionista's delight
The blues, the hues,
The green, the white,

The bunnies, the birds,
The complimentary words:
"Thank you, Auntie."
"Slow & steady."

"Pretty spring dress."
The buffet–the best!
The cute crafts fair
With the Hawaiian flair

The Coachella in bed
Isle never forget!
Aloha mana
Ohana, Kalaka

Funky Monkey

Kapa'a, Kauai, HI
Is a big city
For this hillbilly!

Leaving town
Gassing up
Going home.

Squeezing into traffic
Back and forth
Green light go!

Was in reverse!
Actually punched it!!
Rix in a snit!!!

Outta here, Dallas Alice

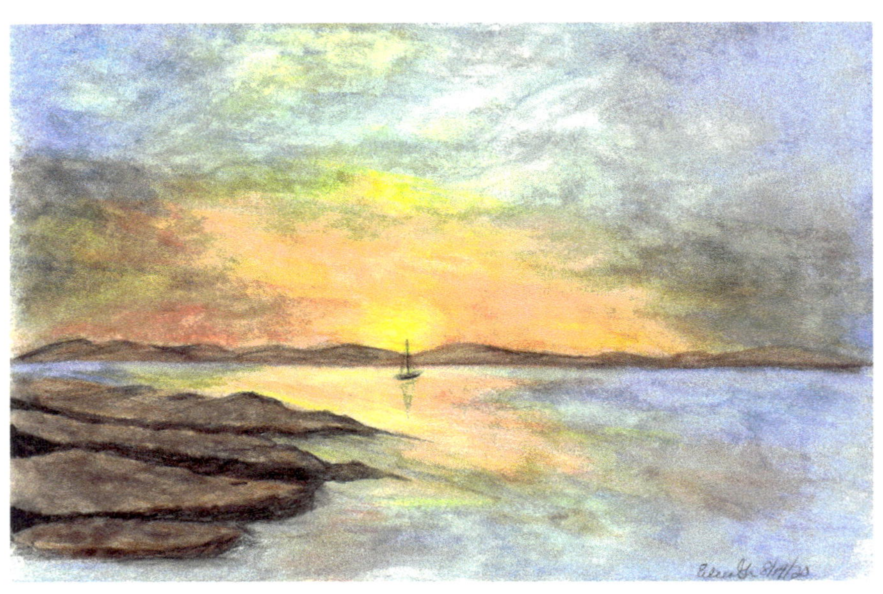

April In Kona

Aloha from Kona
Birthday on the beach
34 years sober
As a judge each

Never been better,
Never had it so good
Enjoying the Big Island
Like Nancy knew we would

How I wish she were here
Especially this year
Hillary's getting married
To Joe Oliveira

It's all about legacy
Mother to daughter to niece
For the stars we reach
& party on the beach!

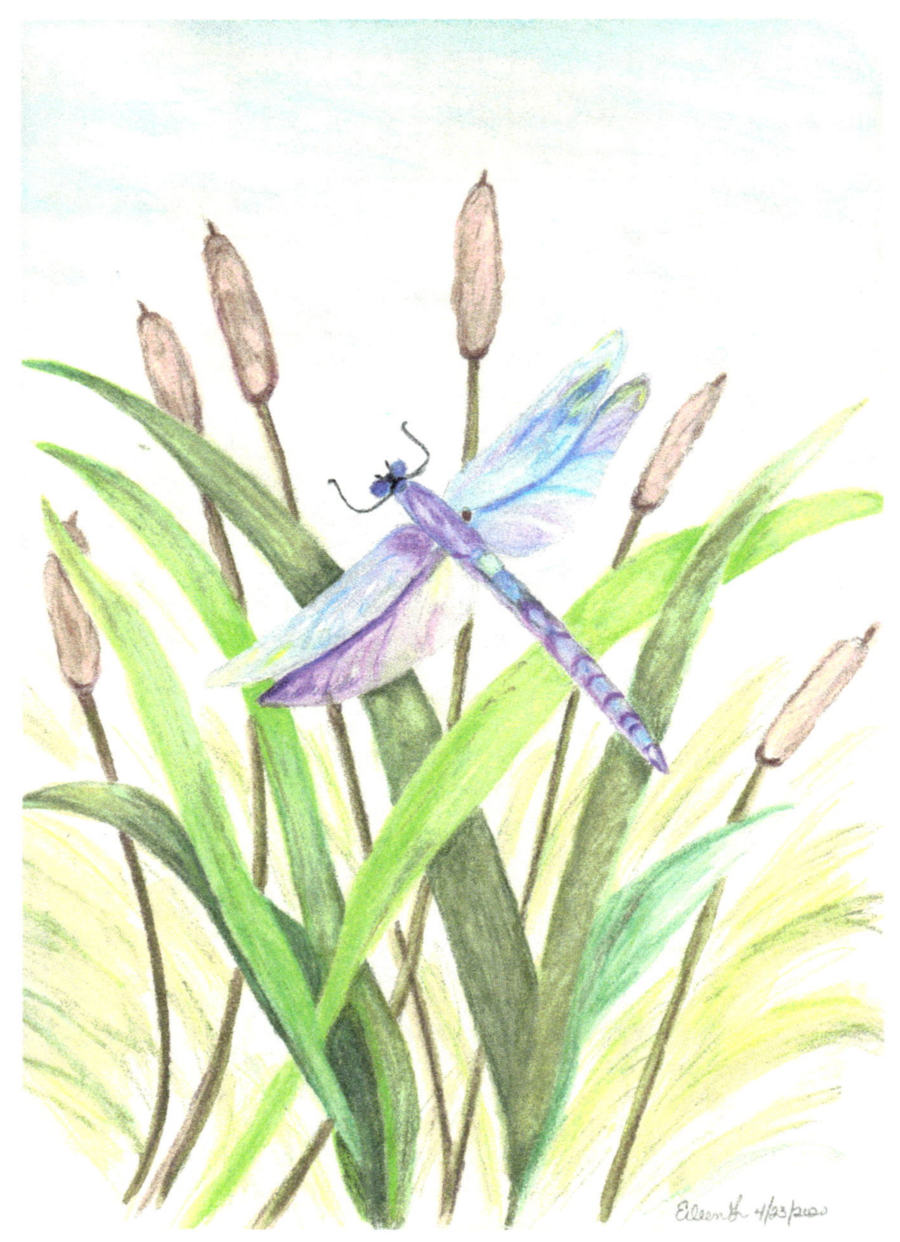

4/20 (Tobe-Star)

A giantess dragonfly
Comes up out of her plume
She only see Kila view
In her green muumuu

Kona coffee
Taste like popcorn
Sippin' it munchie-munchie
On our way to the southern horn

Earth without art
Is only "eh"
It's finally 4/20
All day today!

The Hawaiian Hipfloss
Is the new dance craze
May Kiki keep rockin' it
For days upon daze!!

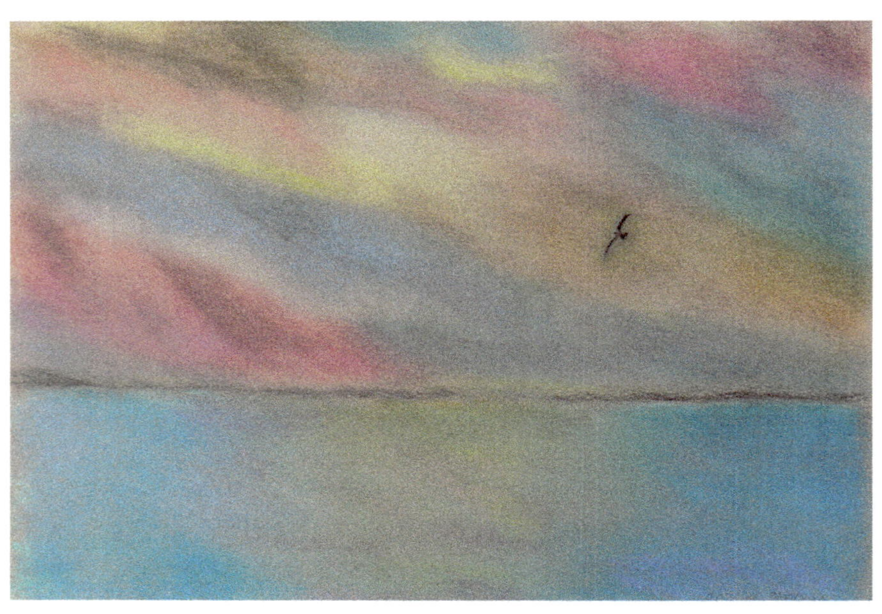

Dallas Ann Aloha

Holed up on Hawaii
Only me
Pure unadulterated glee
In everything I see

Cozy jacuzzi
Cute coverup
Mauna Kea, Mauna Loa, Hualalai, Kohala & Kilauea
Got any sacrifices to offer up today?

Dad is guiding me
Mom is supporting me
Rick is loving me
All from afar

No TV
No one to see
No place to be
And no car!!!

Dallas Ann In Paradise

Aloha all alone
Sleeping diagonal on the bed
In my Kona home
Trying to clear my head

Felt the velvet embrace,
Warm sunshine on my face,
Starting each day with grace
Oh, how I love this place!

Got coffee & lotsa noodles
Fresh pineapple & cottage cheese
Got all the nutritional foods
A determined writer needs

A fully-loaded 3-month-old Boeing
Flew south so as to skirt an El Nino
"Bumpiest ride I've ever been on,"
Said Purser Mike who looked like Rob Lowe!

Africa

Good morning Arusha

Good morning Richard

Good morning Iruth

Good morning Monkey Family

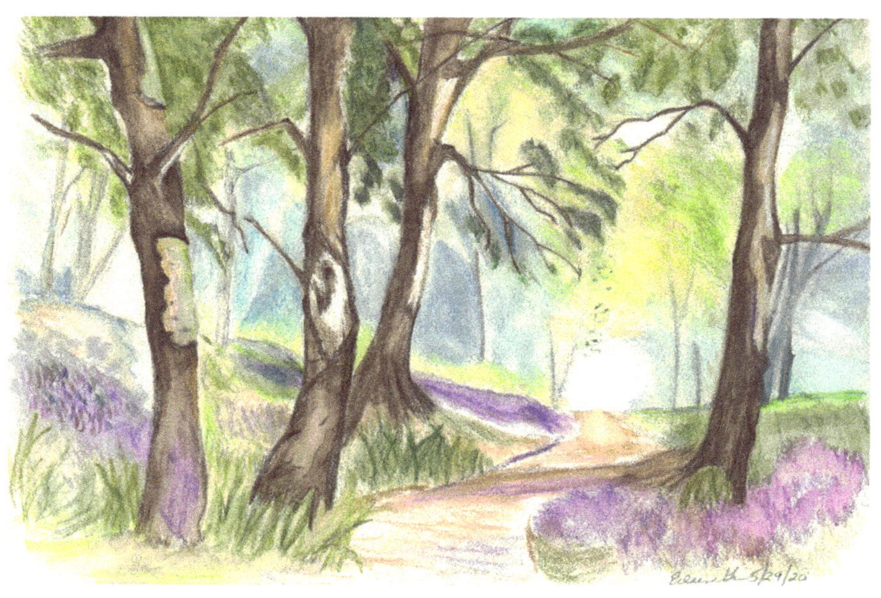

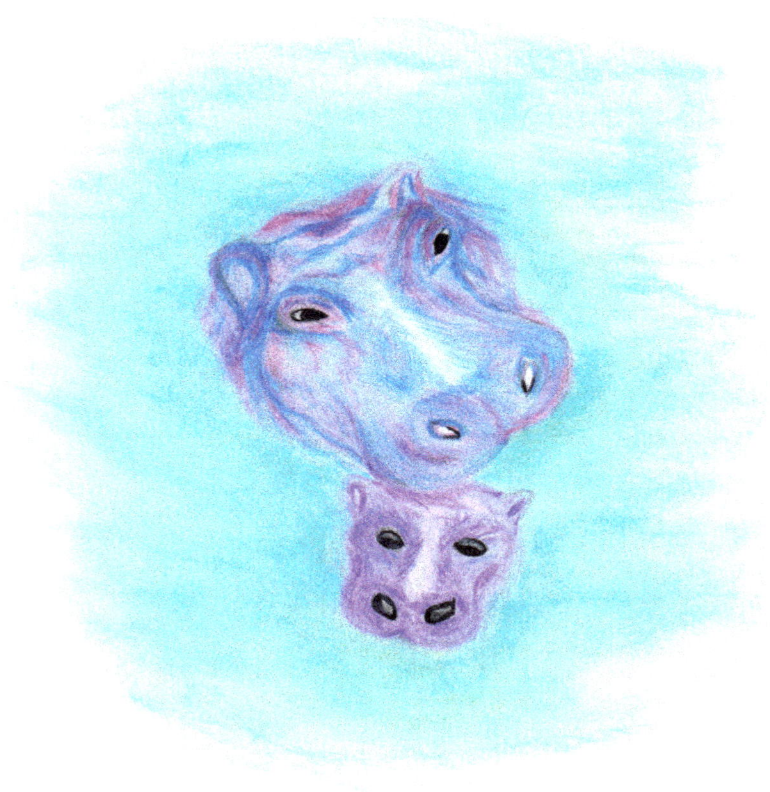

Ngorongoro Crater

Paradise of herbivores
Kingdom of the lions
Saw a couple kaka pride
Cross the crater among us

Dazzles of zebra
Hippopotamus pond
Declaring our love
Was beyond the beyond

Water bottles in bed
Warming our butts
All night long
For all of us

Wading in the pool
While Happy Abby swam
Talking the birds & bees
With my new-found little friend

Ashes To Ashes

Tanzania
Soul stirring
My mania
Was purring

Tire rubber
Sandal soles
Masai walkers
On the side of the road

Natural resources
Minerals
The people, the water
The flag unfurls

African powder
Creates the Ghosts
Of Kilimanjaro
Dust to dust!

Asante Africa

I miss it already
Missed seeing Kilimanjaro
It's so elusive
Always covered in snow.

It was clear & visible
from the bottom to the top
the day before
we took off.

Our last day
was pouring down rain;
therefore Kibo
remained a no-show.

Oh, but the rhinos,
we saw a couple of those!
But, alas, Kilimanjaro
not so.

Cowboy Christmas Limerick

Greetings from Las Vegas
We're here for Cowboy Christmas,
Did a little bar hopping
And lots of Christmas shopping.
Holiday Love, Denise & Dallas

Dramamine

I once took a trip to Nantucket.
I cannot believe where God stuck it.
Way out in the sea,
We traveled with glee,
My head the whole time in a bucket!

Burien Boys Limerick

There once was a princess named Chris
Who each Burien Boy did miss
And her husband, Fair Tim
No one missed him
Till time for good-byes ~ Anonymous

Beach Limerick

Eat, sleep, party at the beach
Seconds, days, for a whole week
Hysterical laughter
Happily ever after,
Tomorrow back to the desert heat

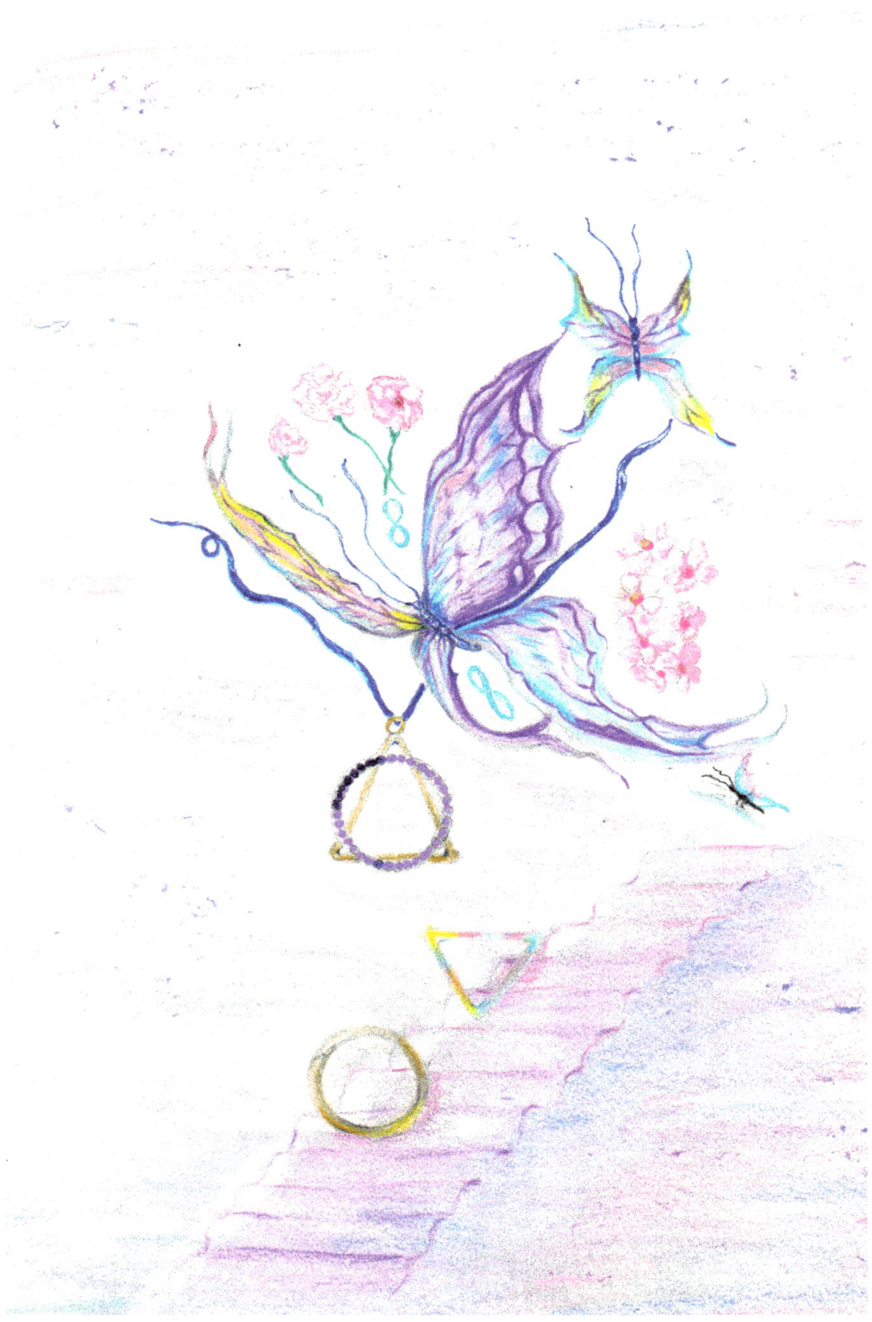

Chapter Ten

Sobriety

Full Circle

I did my drinking
In the backyards and bars,
On the beaches and boulevards
Of San Diego County

I did my time for that pouting
In the San Diego County
Jail

My recovery started
In the church rooms and clubs,
The Fellowship Halls and hubs
Of Alcoholics Anonymous

I do my time today
In meetings of AA
No fail

Ego

I know a place to go
Where a girl can resume
Her self-esteem
And a boy can forgo
His ego.

She gets fueled
With God's love.
His ego gets placed
In God's hands.

E-G-O
Edging God out.
Ego, out.
Let Him in.

Start at the heart
Meet in the middle,
Balance till the end

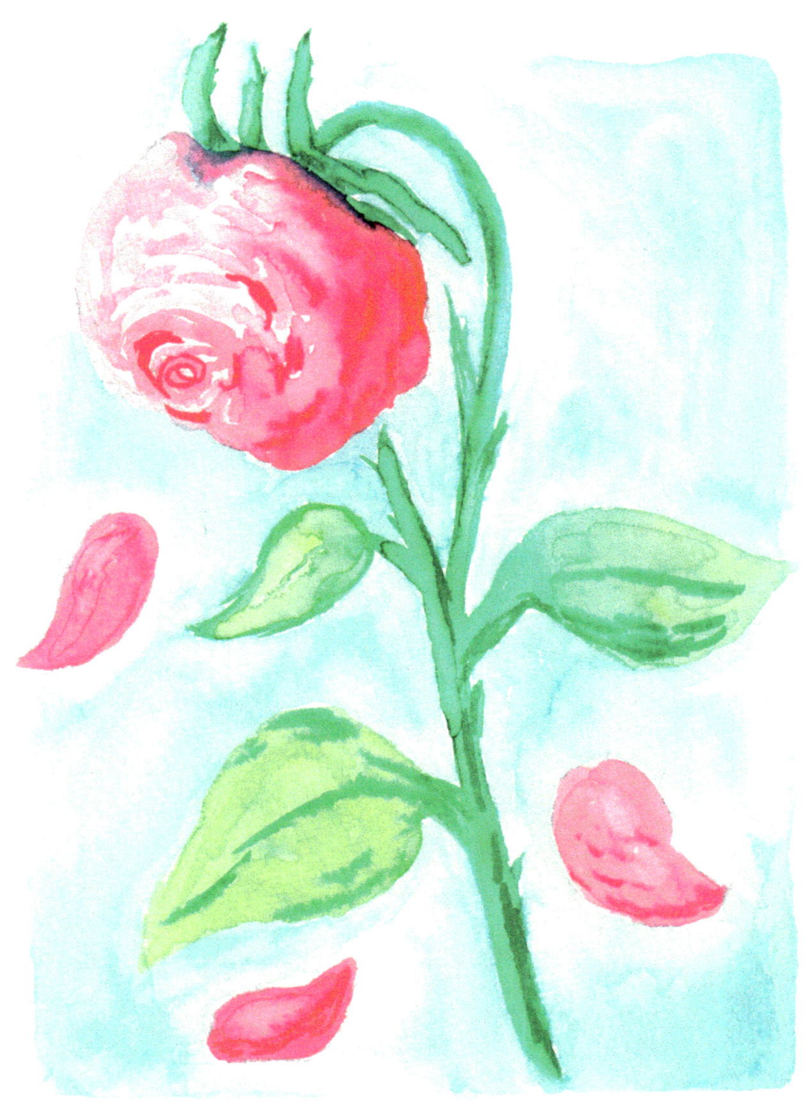

Sorry

I surrender,
I'm sorry,
I quit.
You win.

Please,
Don't ever
Use me
Again.

Until
You're willing
To recognize
"Amends,"

(Step 9)
I'm afraid
Our relationship
Dead ends

Dear Bill

Dear Bill,
2-12-02
I'll be
Thinking about you

Keep it simple
A day at a time
I hope you like
My AA rhyme

Keep the plug
Securely in the jug
I am going to
Miss your mug!

Remember the Love
And God above!
Think, Think, Think,
And just don't drink

Dear Uncle Bill

Welcome to California,
The Keep it Simple state,
The Take it Easy territory,
The land of Live and Let Live,

Where applause abounds,
Where sobriety reigns supreme,
And were Bill is King,
Yea AA!

Happy you're here,
Kudos for coming,
From Dallas Ann E.,
Happy, Joyous & Free!

Dallas Ann To Karen Ann

I love her,
She loves me.
I talk to her,
She talks to me.
I'm willing to go to any lengths for her,
She's willing to go to any lengths for me.
We are mentor and mentee.

I listen to her,
She listens to me.
I learn from her,
She learns from me.
I'd go to hell and back for her,
She'd go to hell and back for me.
We are sponsor and sponsee.

I resent her,
She resents me.
I tell on her,
She tells on me.
We do this dance one day at a time,
And our relationship is like a fine wine:
Young and musty,
Velvety and lusty

I apologize to her,
She apologizes to me.
I forgive her,
She forgives me.
She is my pigeon,
AA is my discipline,
Sweet and simple,
Glamorous and powerless!

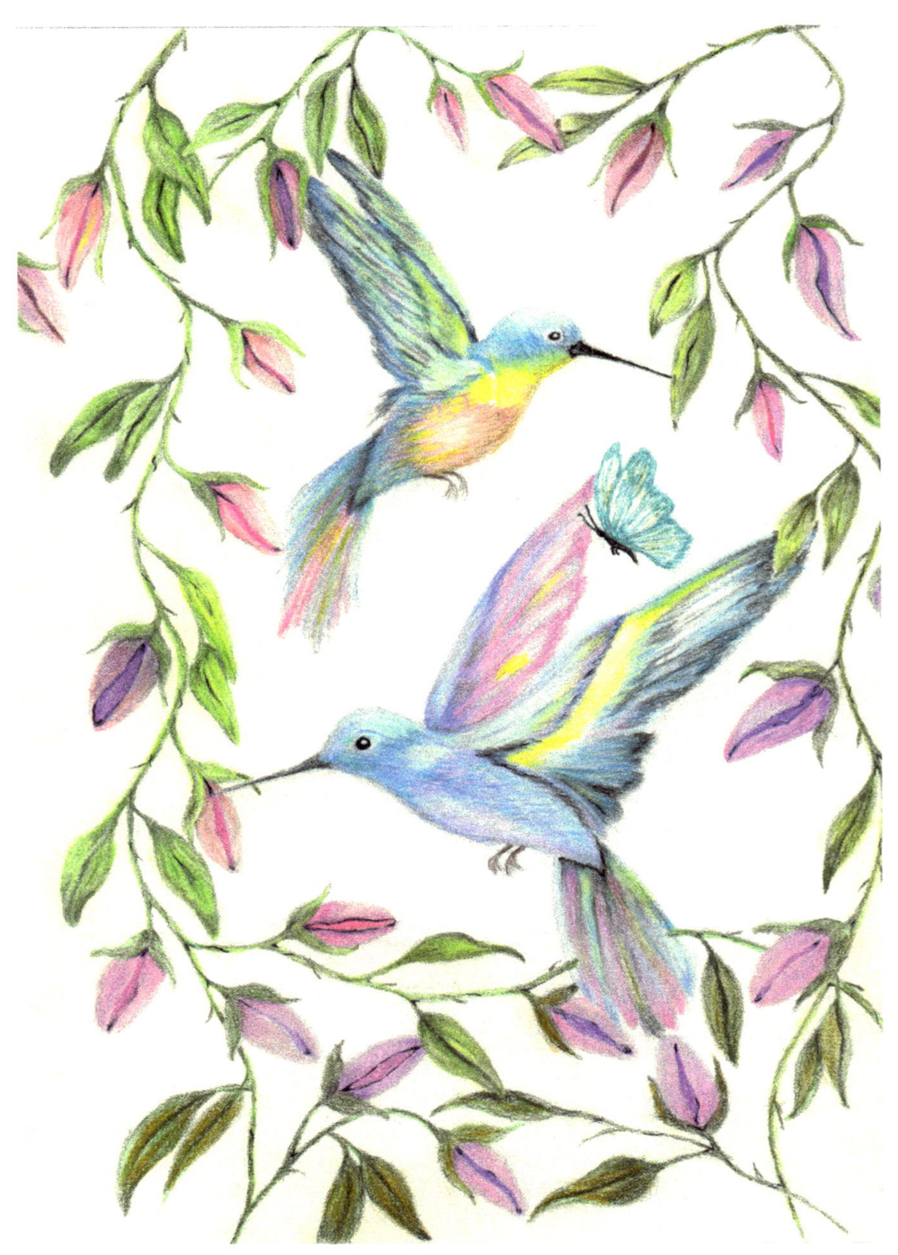

Seven Years Sober

Seven years sober
Just the other day
Saw some old friends,
Wanted to stay.

Loving embraces,
Kisses on the cheek.
Thank you, God!
What a wonderful week.

I'm so glad to be
On my good side again.
Was looking without;
Found it within.

Depression, despair,
What a terrible waste.
Love and happiness
Is a much better place!

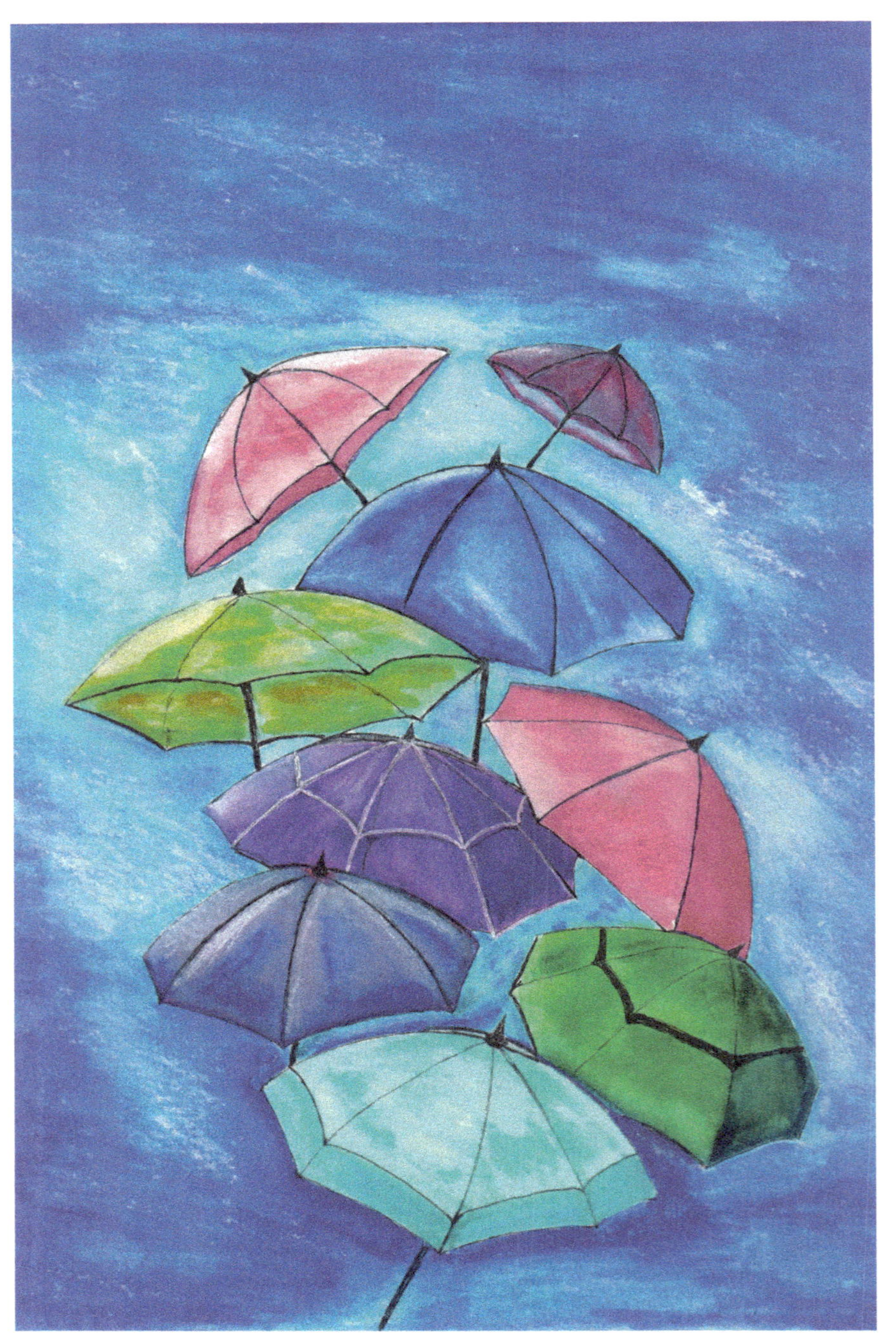

Sobriety

Sobriety is my baby
A precious gift from God

She requires my attention
24 hours a day

She needs to be nurtured
On a daily basis

I have a baby
Her name is Sobriety

She cheers me up
She can tie me down

Our bond is for good
One day at a time

Sure Surrender

I don't care
What people think
'Cause I am here
And I don't drink!

I don't care
What people say
'Cause I don't drink
Just for today!

I don't care
What people do
'Cause I don't drink
And I love you!

I don't care
How people act
'Cause I don't drink
And that's a fact!

Jeff's Poem

Give me a rule
And I'll break it

Show me a step
And I'll take it

Hand me a drink
And I'll forsake it

Grant me sobriety
And I'll make it.

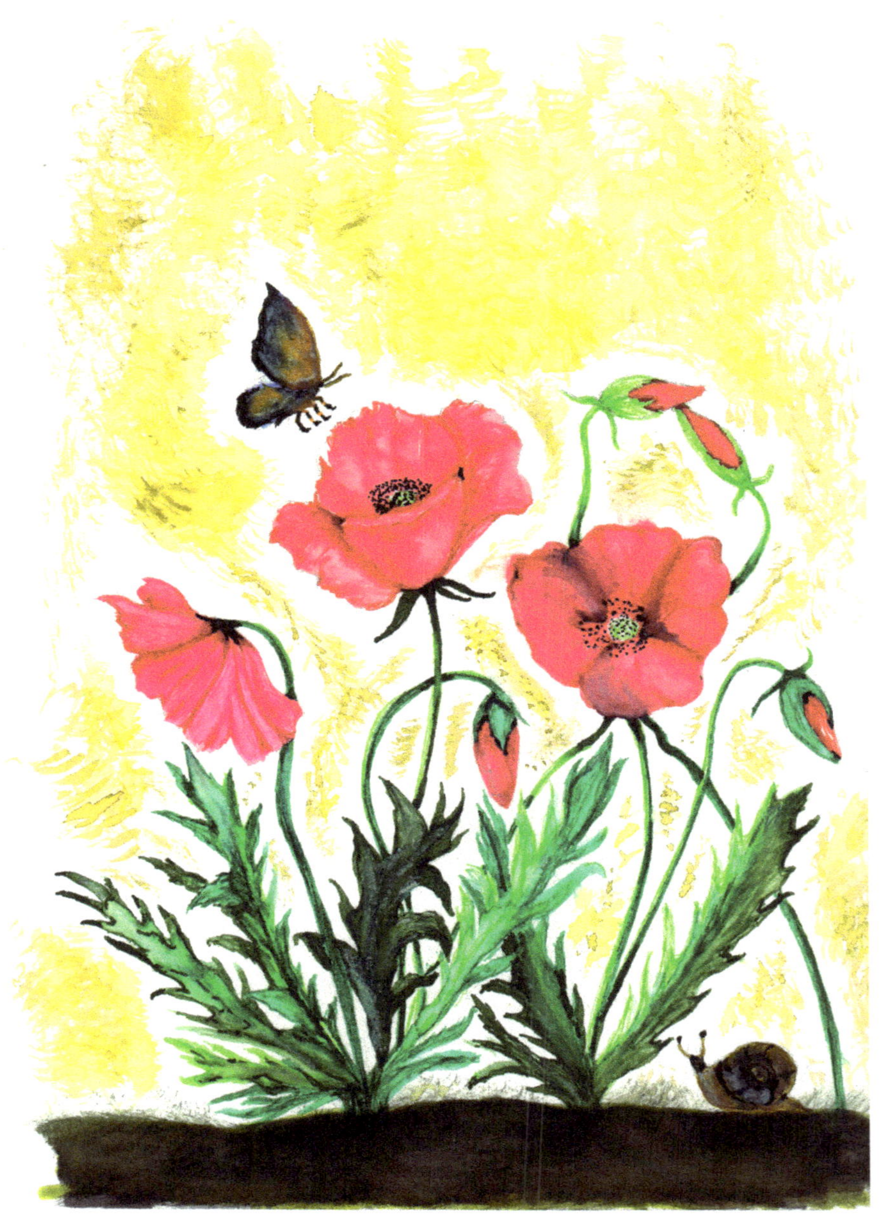

San Diego Smiles

San Diego smiles,
Smooches on the street,
A handshake and a hug
For every one you meet

The sun was shining blue,
And friendly was the hue,
Grateful was the place
On every body's face.

Meetings were the best
For this enchanted guest.
Beaches were the key
To summer serenity.

Oh let this feeling last,
This impression linger on,
Healing what was cast
By the spirit of anon.

Keep Coming Back

I awaken in a warm/cool sweat
From a long, long time ago
When tall bearded men roam the land
Mysterious places only I know

Mother is special, friends are dear
Flirtations are all around
Light on her feet, sugar and spice
The temptations, they do abound.

Reality is slowly checking in
From a splendid, needed vacation
I sit and wait knowing full well
That I have this inclination

To write, to read, to learn once more
To serve on a daily basis,
To keep coming back and check in on
Your smiling, loving faces

Anonymous

Anonymous:
No one knows
My secret spiritual
Principles

Openness:
So vulnerable
Soft & pliant
Susceptible

Honesty:
I swear to God
I tell the truth
Then wink & nod

Willingness:
Is the key
To a life
With dignity

Annette

Annette
Liked her athletics
She knew the score
That's what I asked her to be my sponsor for

It was later in my sobriety
It was my AA birthday
So I gifted myself
With AA's top shelf

So sweet and sublime
She had the time,
And her AA story
Of Beverly Hills glory,

Her family life
Her domestic song
Her legacy
One day at a time long

This Is HOW It Works

I'll be Honest
You have an Open mind
And we'll all be Willing
To grow along spiritual lines.

7:00 A.M. Smoking

You are the hard core
And they are the sweet meet
From the fruit of the tree
That feeds me my sobriety

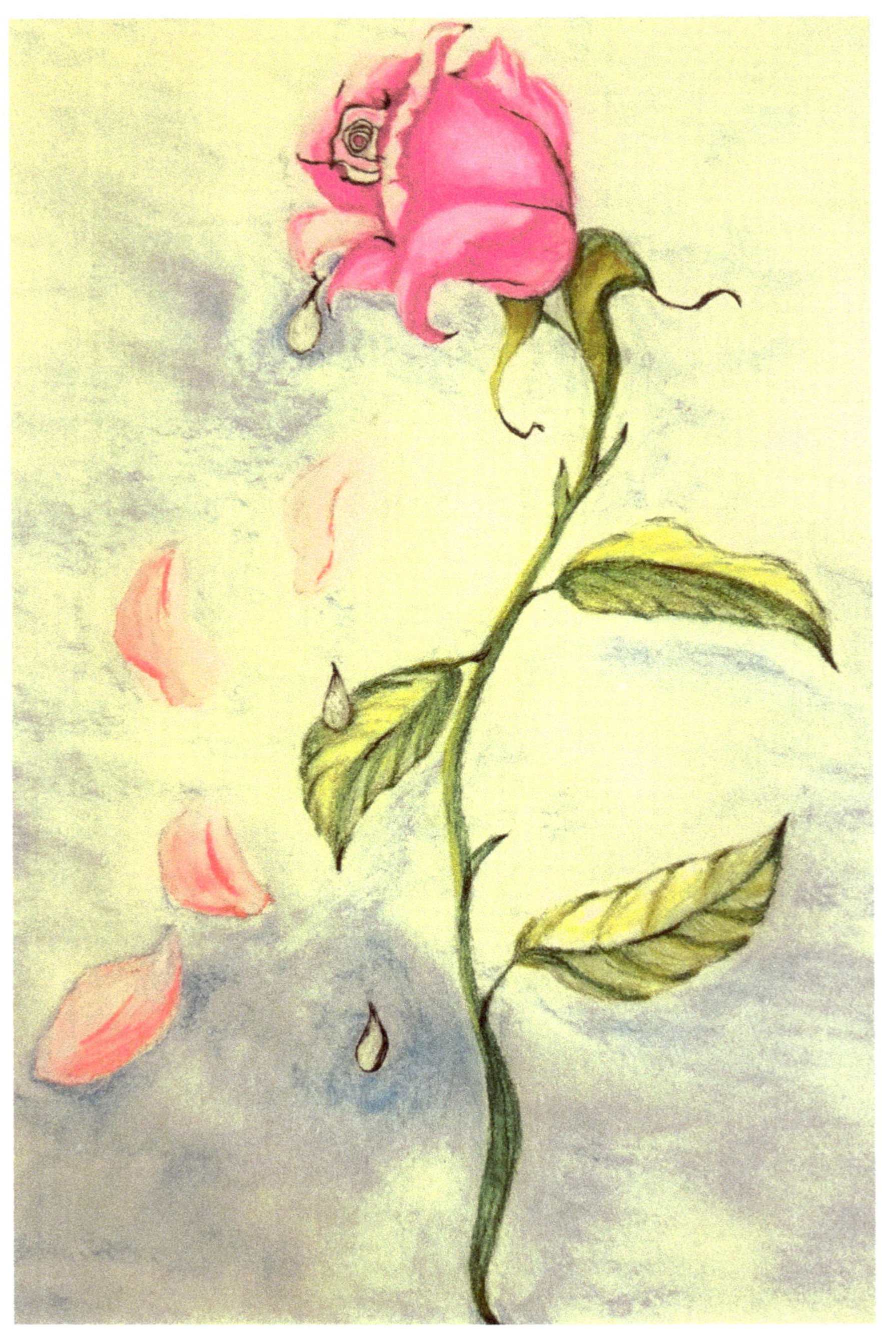

Chapter Eleven

Remembrances

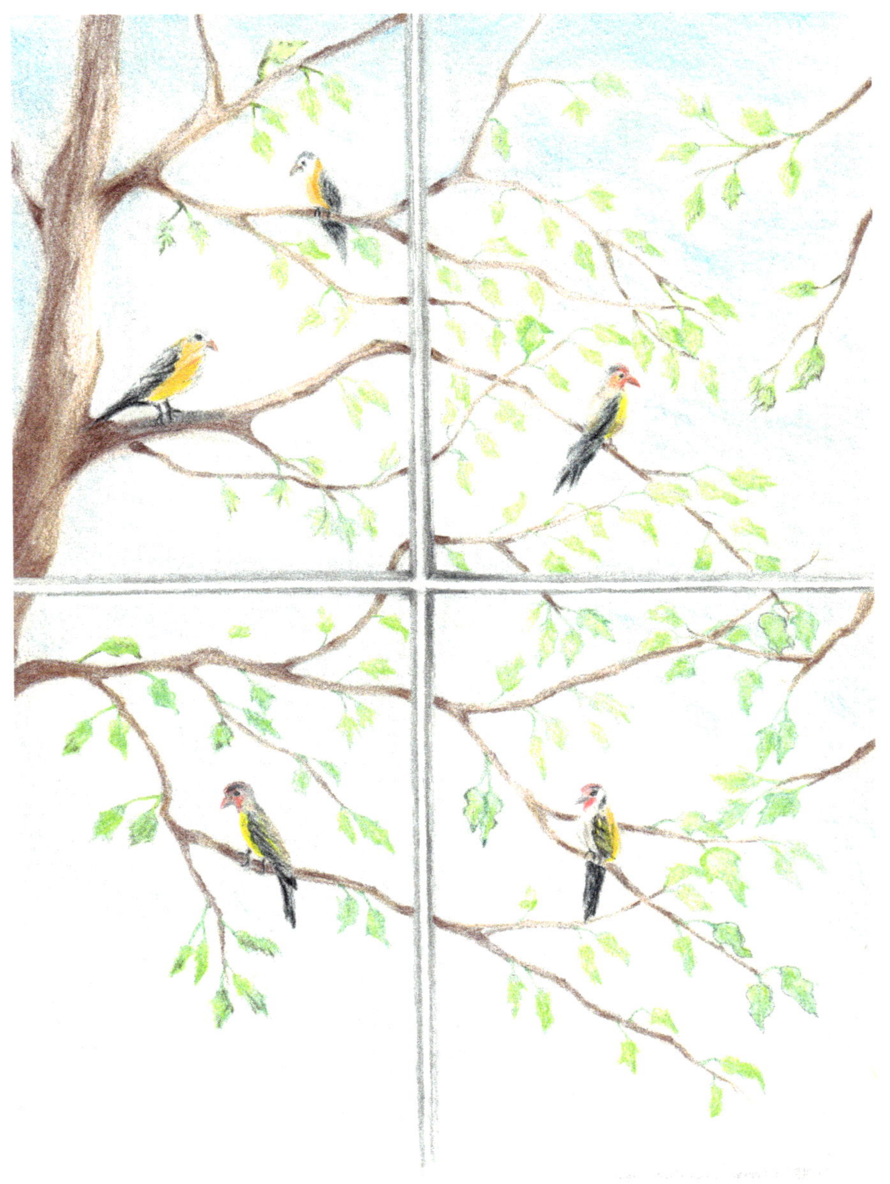

Birds

Mourning birds are singing
In the middle of the night;
I sleep in fits and worry:
Will she be all right?

Morning birds are chirping
In the beautiful sunlight.
I wake in peace and wonder.
She will be all right.

Don's Obit

Don's obit
From a friend's beloved
A life well lived
He was wanted, needed & loved

Our most generous realtor
Whose opinions always uplift
Gave us a garage door opener
As a house warming gift!

Loyal son, brother, spouse,
Father, grandfather, friend
Always had the coolest cars
A great neighbor, a beautiful man.

May the memory be blessed
Of Brenda and Don
In peace may they rest
Love's legacy lives strong

When I think of Don,
I think of food and shelter
And how important it's become
To take care of your partner

Valentine's Day dinners
Fourth of July on the beach
Christmas gift boxes
Full of sweet treats

I'll always remember
His little-boy laugh
And I'd ofter wonder:
Can you adopt a dad?

I'll never forget
What he last said to me
He imparted his best
To us all specially

Their Last Date

On October 30,
2019,
Julia Ann Erwood,
Had a date with her king

At 10:00 p.m.
She met him in heaven
She was not late
For that date with her mate

He was a WWII Sub Vet
She, a goddess of the domestic
They had 3 boy descendants
2 judges & an architect

They danced the golden streets
After her final sweet surrender
Their love was so neat,
So true & so tender

Teacher

Like my mother
I was a daughter,
and like her mother
learned: I taught her.

Teaching
was my parents' gig.
Reaching
is a child's thing.

For the sink
For the bookshelf
To the stars
Towards their best self

Kindergarten
through twelfth grade
what a feature
Teacher made!

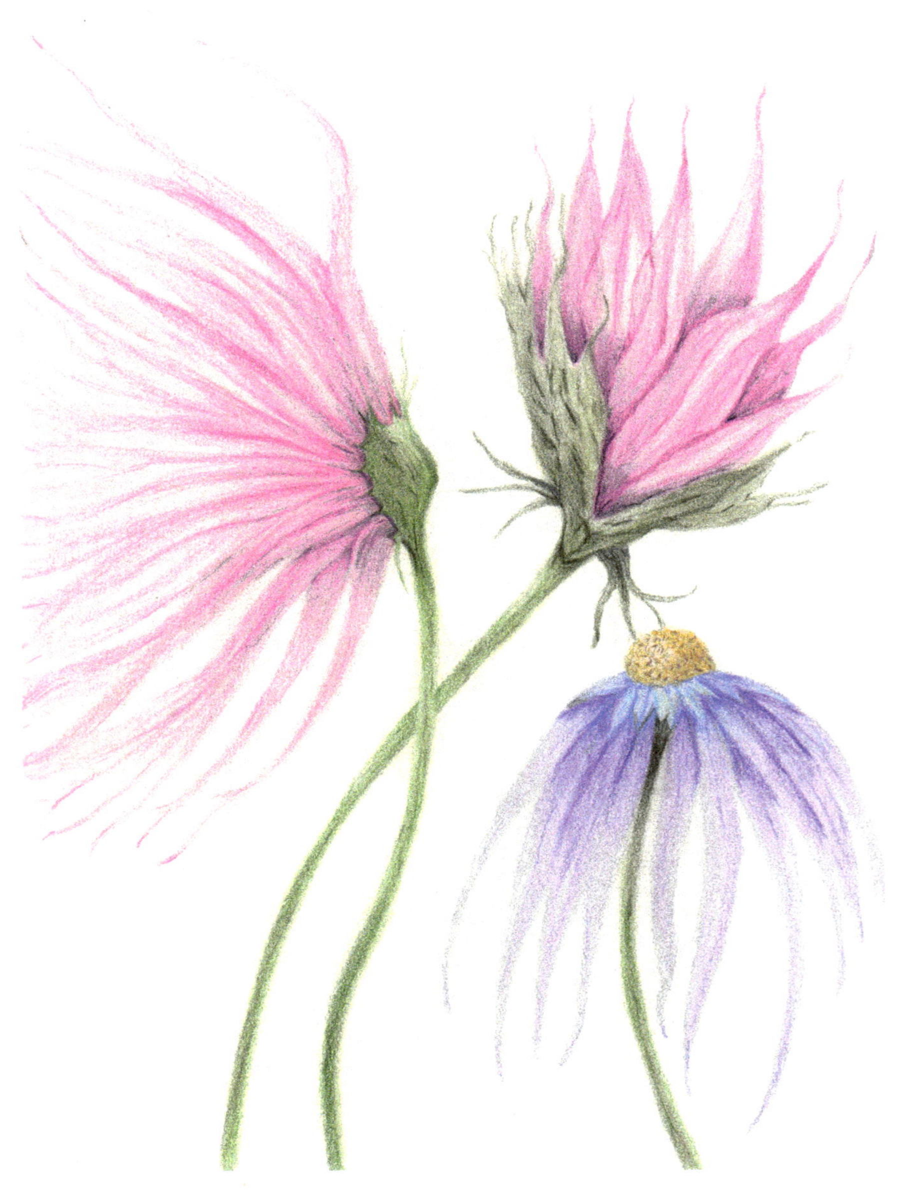

The Gary Trilogy

Gary On

I felt like a princess
Seated next to a king
At a state dinner
The night of the
Performance

Colleagues, friends
Gave respect
To the gentle man
In the silk coat
Nonchalance

Humbly hurting
We carried on.
We courtiers
Of law & love
Stand a chance

The Shadow

The shadow
Of your soul
Is big as
San Jacinto,

As long as
Palm Springs,
As dark as
Brown-green.

The most
Beautiful thing
I've ever seen

Is the shadow
Your soul cast
On San Jacinto

A Fine Example

Gracious Gary
As good as they get
You taught me
Courtroom etiquette

You taught me
The law of man
You taught me
Dallas Ann

I'll miss your kisses
Your greeting with grace
Your joy, your laughter
The heart on your face.

You are the law
We all should follow
A fine example
Of love of life

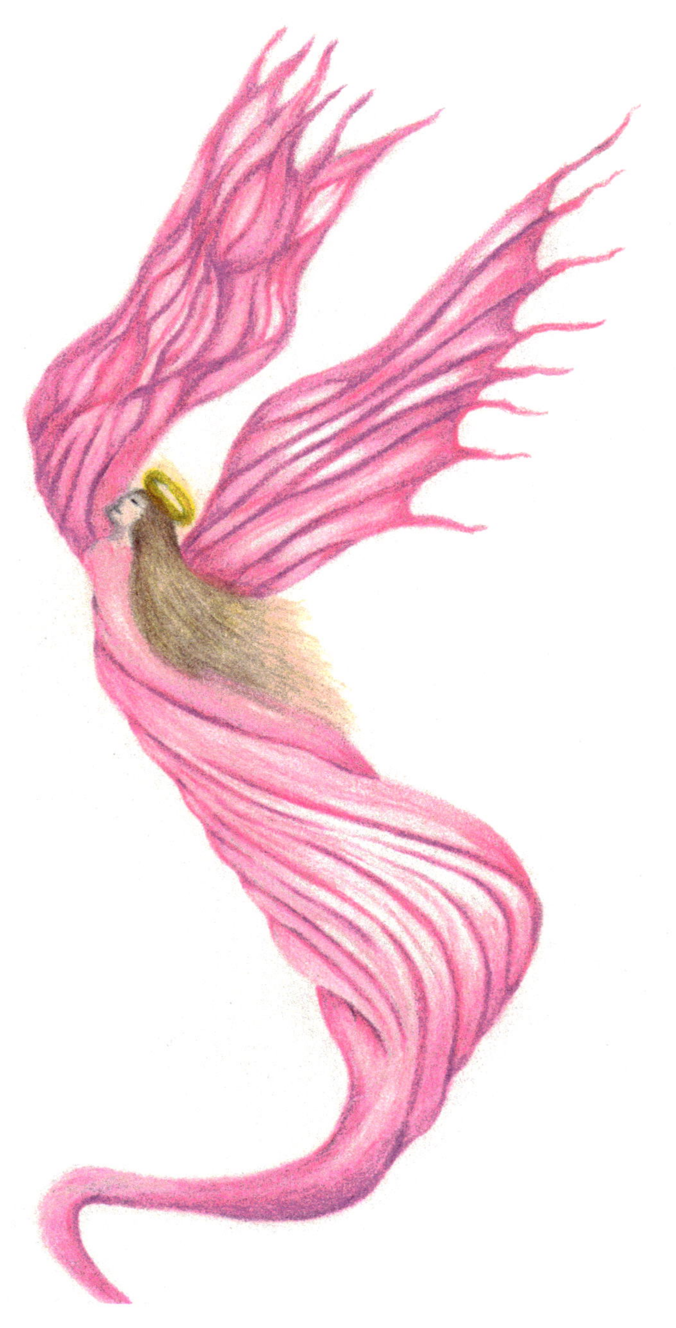

Angel

Last night I was so inspired
Today I am so very tired
I actually saw an angel

Flying too close to the ground
Its hair flapping ‘round
Its gown in the wind

Its halo bright and yellow
It kissed the earth so mellow
It’s LIFE we can’t rescind!

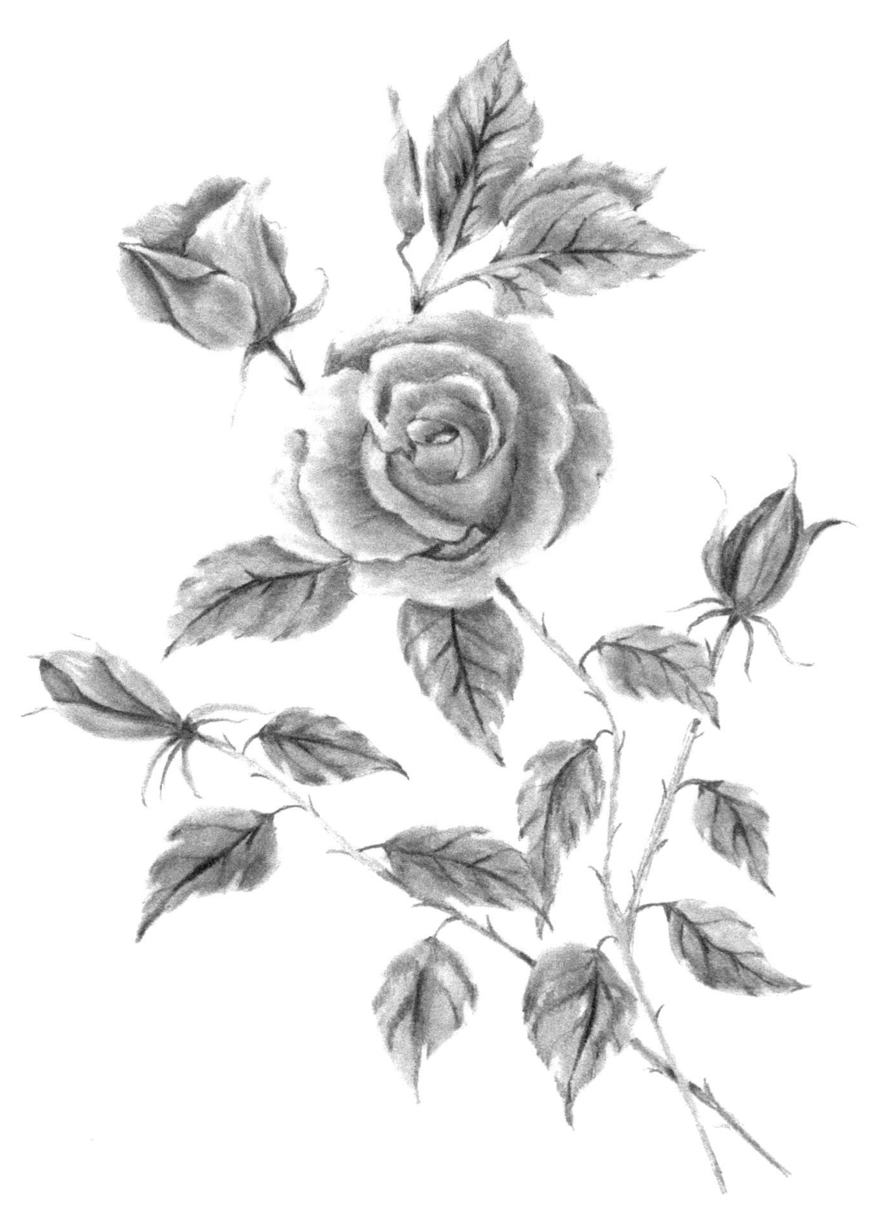

Tom Douglass

Thank you for marrying us
Tom Douglass
And all the pool parties
So joyous

All the funny jokes
Quite hilarious
The nice compliments
So gracious

And the working together
So laborious
The many concerts
So melodious

The sweet gifts
So generous
All your life
Just so dignified

Tom Douglass (Continued)

For all the love and happiness
And the dinners so fun and delicious
All the hugs, truly scrumptious,
Much love from Rick and Dallas

The Day Royalty Died

We pulled into
The Queen of Siam
And heard the news
Of Princess Diana.

We ordered Thai
While Lady Di
Clung to life
Then, sadly, died.

First serious, then grave
Then finally dead.
Visions of princes
Crying in my head.

Innocence, beauty,
Brand-new starts.
Graceful royalty,
Queen of hearts.

A wise old woman
She will never be.
Her beauty will remain
Through all eternity.

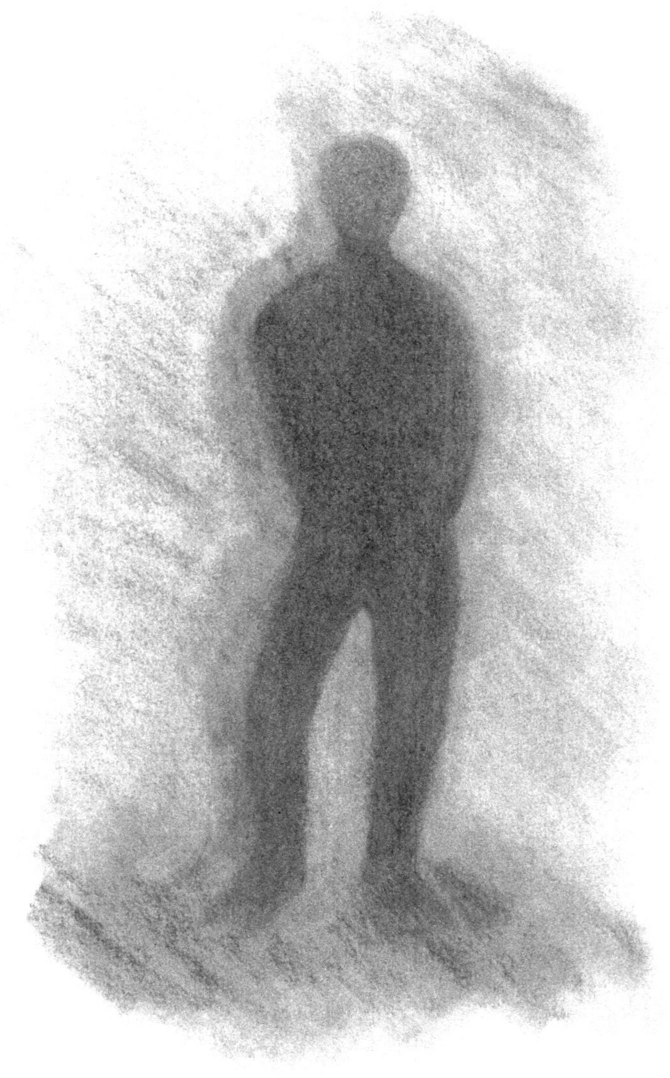

Statues

Eulogy for
Two friends
Who both died
At September's end

We in California
Erect statues to
Men like the
Both of you

Tall, strong & tan
Bearded men
With kind eyes
And cute smiles

They ask you how you are
And you take a little piece
Of their extra-large heart
And say, "Never better, thank you!"

Statues (Continued)

Such is the love story

Between Dallas Ann

And her two adored friends

Eric & Gary

Halloween 2015

Bill Greenley
Was the epitome
Of service with a smile
California style

Frank O. Nelson
Was a lion
In this profession
Santa Barbara style

It was Halloween day
I read on a Facebook page
The passing away
Of wisdom and a sage

Two giants
Of court reporting
Two more
To live for

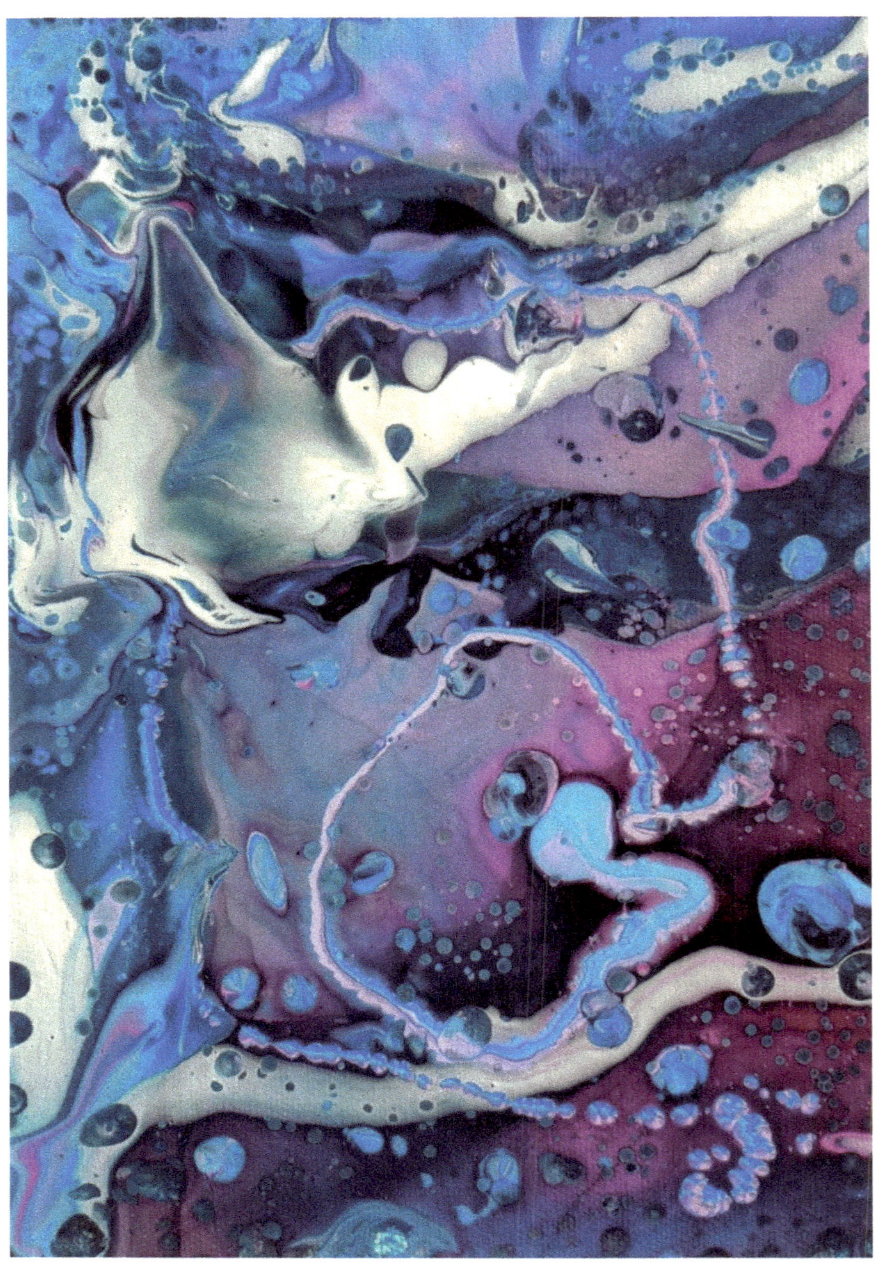

Chapter Twelve

Work

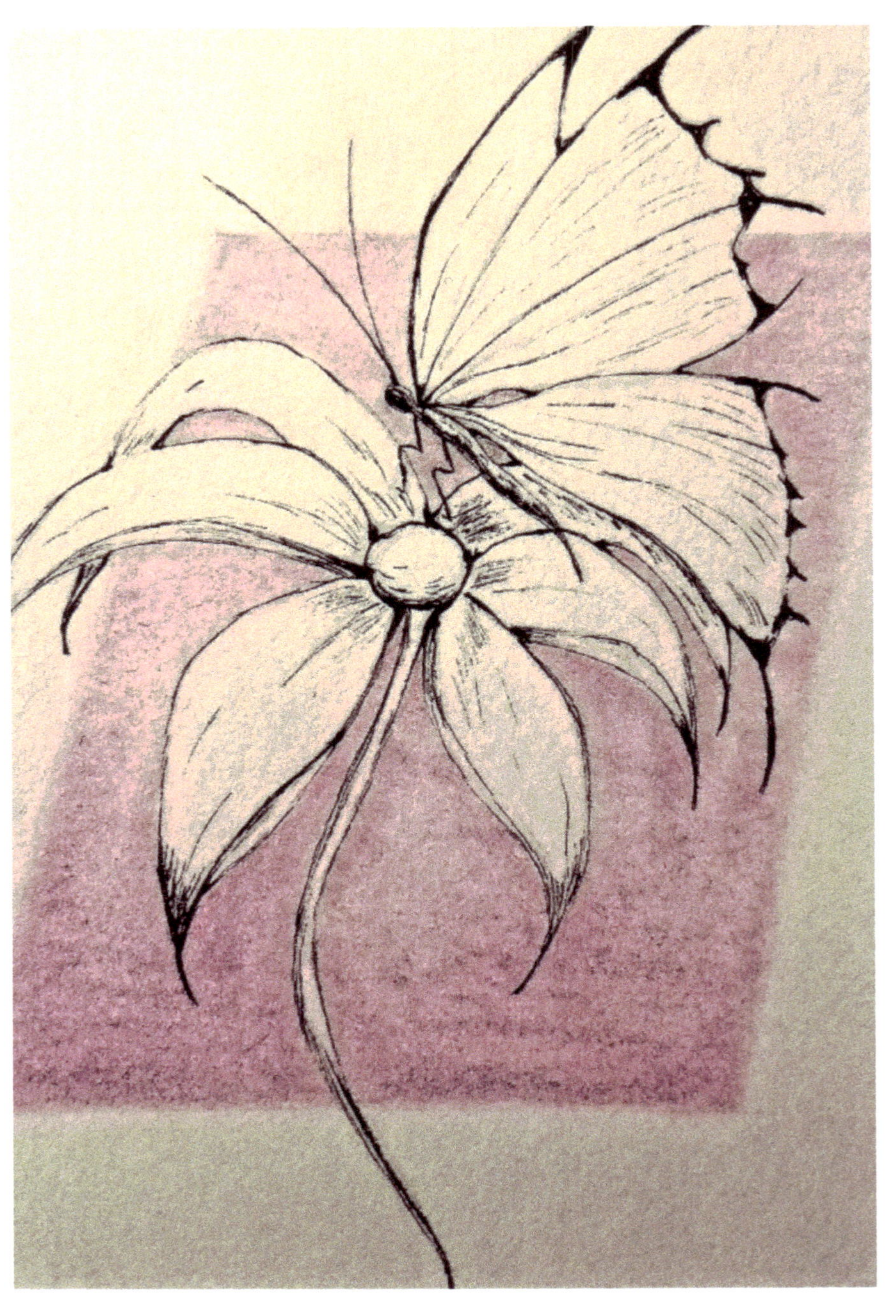

Betty's Retirement

Bye-bye, Betty, we bid you adieu.
The office just won't be the same without you.
There every day, bright and early,
Face and hair, soft and curly.

Thank you for helping us all through the years,
Your understanding talks, your laugh, your tears.
Your attitude about things professional in nature
Has led us to respect your slight but strong stature.

It's time now to leave your chosen profession,
No more lawyers in endless procession
Talking real fast, using five-dollar words.
Say a gracious "Good-bye" to those loquacious herds!

We hope as your retirement years unravel
They're full of friends, relaxation and travel.
Up, up and away; the limit's the sky.
Bye-bye, Betty, butterfly

Doodle

Here I sit, bored to tears,
Waiting for the golden years,
Working hard to pay expenses,
Trying not to sit on fences.

Loving one, loving all,
Waiting patiently for him to call
And when he does, I run to be there
To revel in the happiness we share.

I tell my friends he's just another
Man in my life, kinda like a brother
When, in truth, he is the one.
My dancing days have just begun!

On Being A Court Reporter After A Bad Day

Into each year
of a court reporter's career
two, maybe three, sheer
difficult days must appear.

That's just
the mother lovin'
nature of the job.
Not bad odds.

Oh, No! Barry

Two days down
I hope ten thousand more to go!

Friends and colleagues,
What a great combo!

It's an interesting pleasure
Watching you work, don't you know.

On the ninth day,
He kicked me out the door!

The Brilliant Tyrant
Or
Anatomy Of A Disaster

He's smart
He's funny
His heart
Is cunning;

He demands
Respect
He commands
Neglect

I'm sorry
I'm wrong
The sparing!
So long!!

Once colleagues
Cum friends
Then underling
The END!!!

Grateful

Lucky a lot
Boy, am I hot
What a streak!
What a freak!!

First an all star
Then the CSR
Then U2 tickets
Then a grand gift certificate!

Shopping at Nordies
With twenty-five forties
God is great
I cannot wait!!

I work hard
No holds barred
I've got in made
I'm way overpaid!!!

Mrs. Saska 70th Birthday Poem

Happy, happy birthday, dear, sweet Pauline!
I just can't believe you're only seventeen!!
It's been a long time since I've laid eyes on you.
Nobody serves it up better than you do!!!

I enjoyed growing up with you and yours
Doing all those wonderful restaurant chores.
When it comes to bosses, a better one there ain't.
In my humble opinion, you're truly a saint!

I'll always remember the kindness you showed
The night I ruined a patron's leather coat
By over-pouring water right onto his lap.
Somehow you handled it; I'm grateful for that.

So surprise, sweet Pauline, today is your day!
May many happy returns come cantering your way.
I can't tell you how happy I am to be here
To share in your 70th birthday cheer!

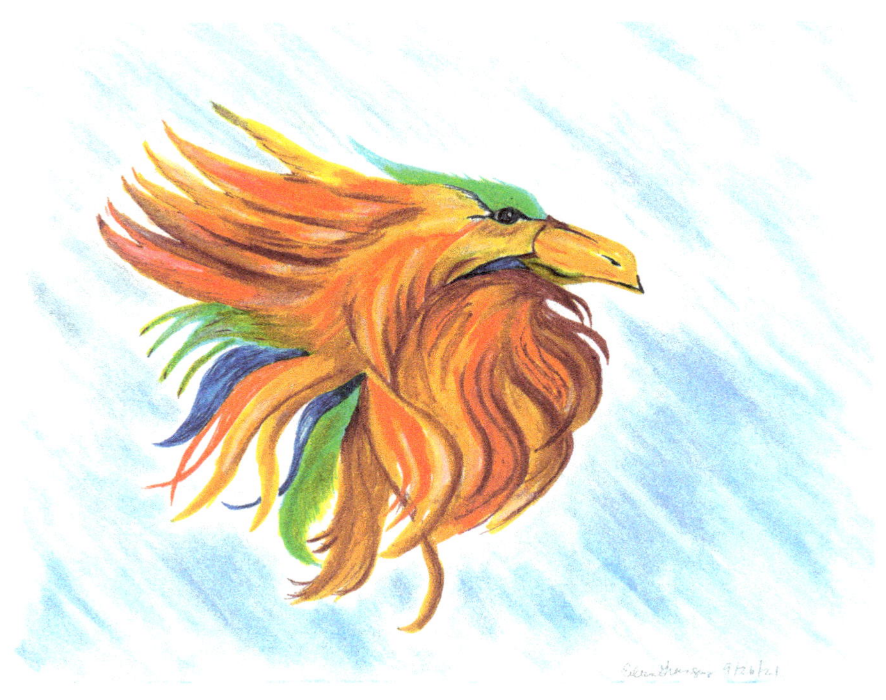

Chapter Thirteen

Politics

Inauguration Day

I woke up and could feel
The healing

Of this Inauguration Day
Immediately.

It was dark and rainy in the desert.
What a blessing.

I donned my custom-made
Sweatshirt for the occasion.

My three take-aways
From this Democracy Day:

Justice, royal blue and I'm boldly optimistic
Restless, Dallas

20th Century America

The aughts were wonderful

The teens were terrible

The 20's were roaring

The 30's were sobering

The 40's were warring

The 50's were soaring

The 60's were spastic

The 70's were fantastic

The 80's were diseased

And the 90's we're at ease

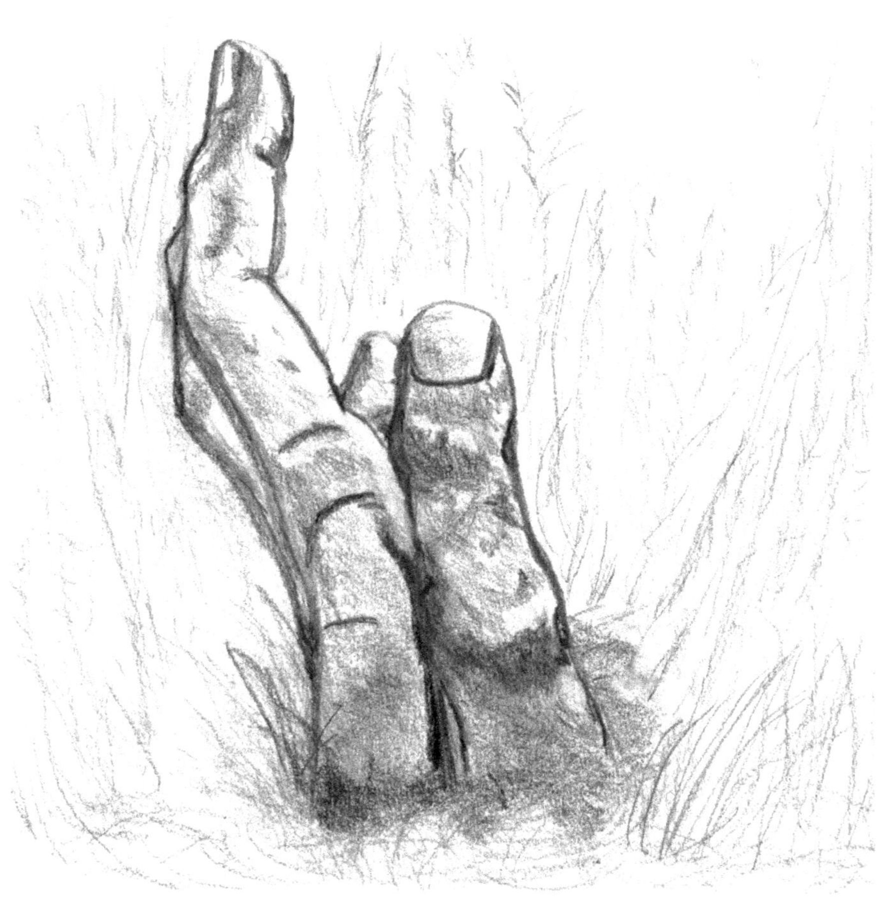

Change Prayer

Aching for change
Hearts breaking for change
Create change
Change, dang it!

Embrace change
Friends for change
The change gang
My change harangue

Inspiring change
Change jangles
Change for kids
Legislate change

Make change
Navigate change
Open to change
Pray for change

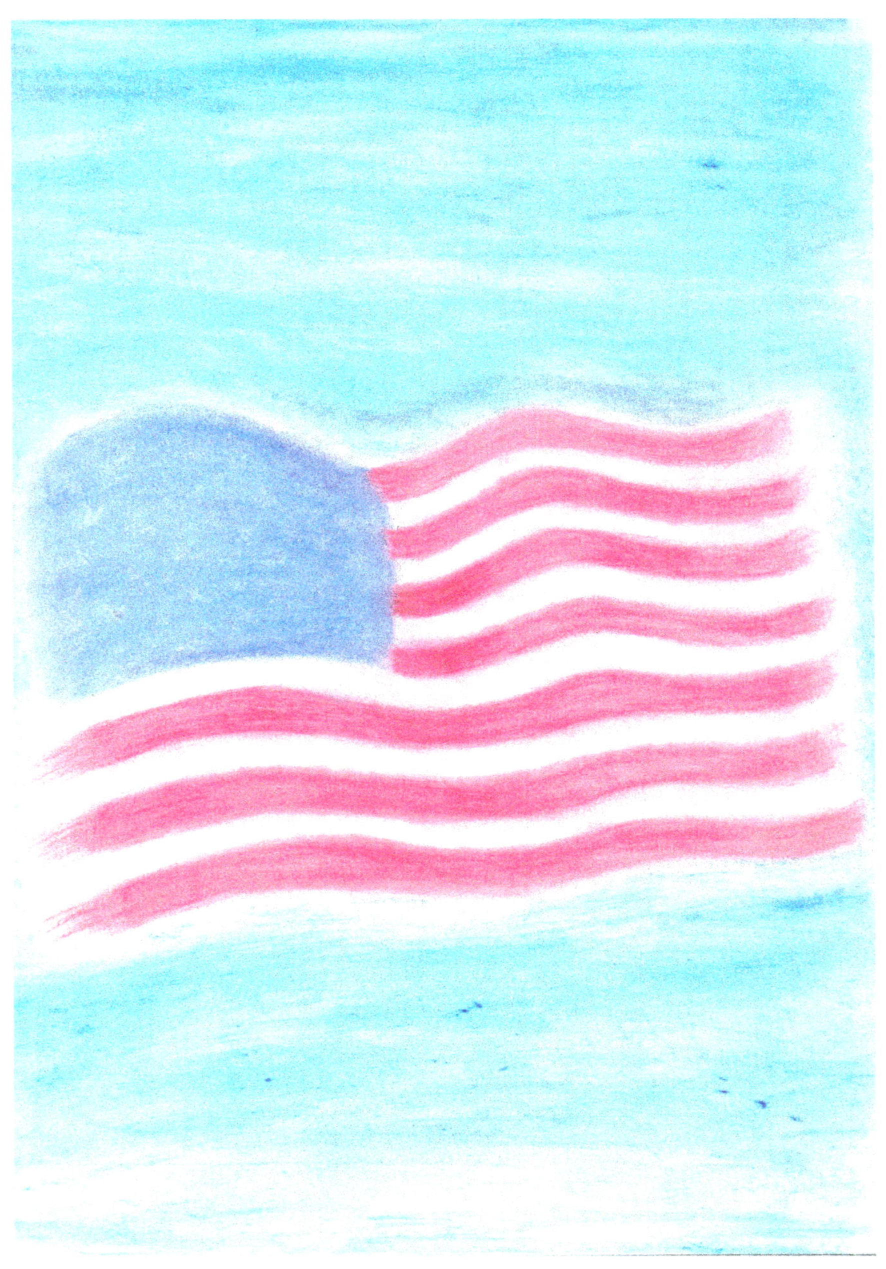

Terrible Tuesday

I love N.Y., and the U.S.A.
Was bombed today
By four of its own
Commercial airplanes: Terrorism!

Lots can happen
In 24 hours
Man's world can crumble
A woman can lose her mind

That's not gonna happen
In the next 24 hours.
We'll get through this
One day at a time

So press on, fear not
And let freedom reign!
Keep the faith; embrace change.
Love is the safest plane

War Metaphors

Tyrannical lamenters
Dictatorial dissenters

Nazis at Nuremberg
4-Star General in my living room!

Territorial offerings
Threatening phone rings

You can all kiss my ass,
Private First Class

Thoughts On An Inauguration

January 22, 2013, 6:36 AM

Having breakfast at
Lowell's Almost Classy
Since 1957
In Pikes Place Market
Seattle, Washington

We caught the last half
Of President Obama's speech.
Kelly Clarkson's rendition
Of My Country Tis Of Thee
Made me cry.

And who was the cute "One Today" poet
Who pronounced "Sierras" and "Colorado"
Like the long-lost Latin lover of my dreams?
Richard Blanco

Home of the brave
Beyoncé belted out
The Star Spangled Banner
And everyone said good-bye

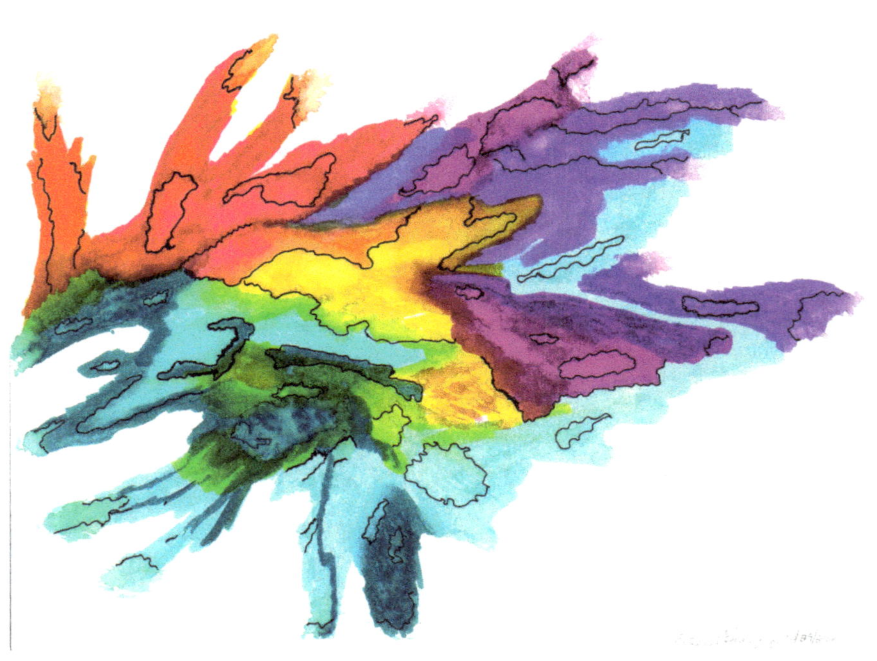

Chapter Fourteen

Poetry To Me

To Dallas

Friends are like books
there are good ones
bad ones, pretty ones
and those with ragged
edges.

Some prefer to stay closed
to be glanced at, then forgotten
on the shelf.
Others are easily understood,
honest. Those we leave
opened.

There are some we've had
since childhood, we go
back to them again and again
But those that never challenge
us we turn away, we cast
aside.

To Dallas (Continued)

Ah but the ones that develop
slowly, draw us in
capture us and hold our attention
They are the ones who touch our
lives. We remember them
forever.

–Eileen

Made You Smile

In 1962
A happy little girl I knew

Always smiling
And friendly too

Dallas is her name
Spreading happiness is her aim

Dear Dallas,
Hoping all is well

Valerie & me are OK.
Hope the poem made you smile.

–Maxine

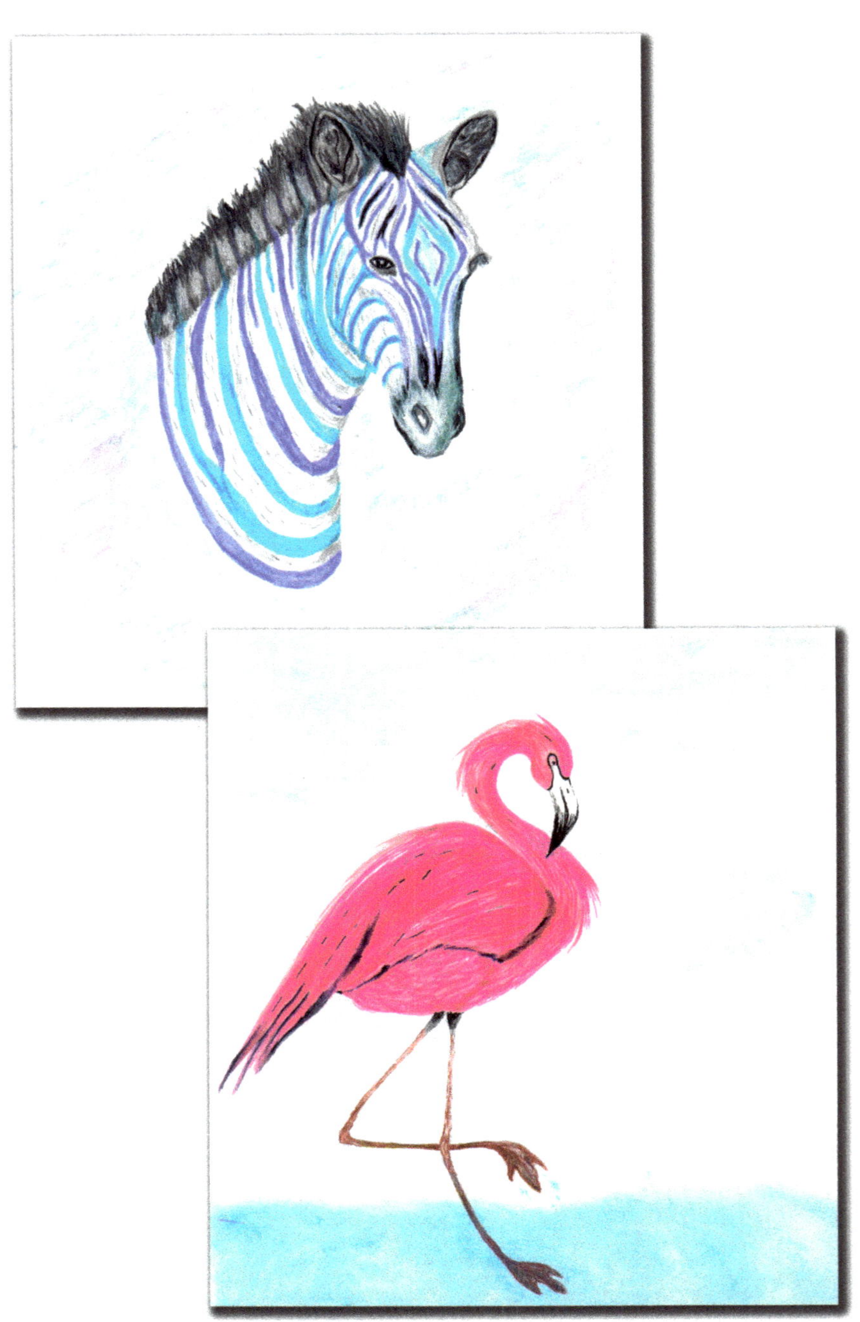

Zebra

To my dear friend Dallas
Who does not reside in
A world that's black & white –
And for that I–nay, the
Planet–is grateful...

–Jan Hawkins

Flamingo – A Haiku

Serene summertime
A swell, strong flamingo hops
At the perfect time

–Donna and Don

Hi Dallas
Merry Christmas '94!

Because you're so clever
With your poems & verses,
I'm giving them a home
For your bestes & worses!

I shopped for the right one,
Oh how I tried.
This one's by black women
But we're all pink inside!

–Lisa

Dallas, Dallas Ann, Dallasie, Dallas E.

Many names,
Many thoughts
Much kindness,
Much love

Continued Joy,
Continued Love
Continued good health,
Continued good travels

These are the things
I wish for you
Plus so much more
Love you my friend

–Rosalind

Dallas Ann E

No matter the measure,
English or metric,
Your personality is electric,
Your taste eclectic,
Perhaps even eccentric.

Your talents abound,
You are fun to be around,
Have both feet on the ground,
A wonderful man you have found
To put your arms around.

Add to above your fantastic intellect,
You are almost perfect,
And your friendship
Is our treasure

–John and Donna

Same Cloth

Life Cheer Leader
With the
Killer Closet

Avid Book Reader
With the
Charged Up Ride

Colors Outside of the Lines
(Lines are Simple Suggestions)

Wife to One
Daughter of Legends
Sister to a Brood
Aunt to a Few
Friend to All

Same Cloth (Continued)

Maker of Memories
Writer of Stories
Citizen of Earth
Supporter of Good

I am lucky to call you
My Aunt Dallas Ann
Cut from the same cloth

–Shannon

A Note Of Friendship

I Love how every time we spend time together,
I always think I should spend more time with you.
I Love that you have been such a good wife to Rick.
I Love your passion for the written word.
I Love that you wrote a book of your Dad's letters.
I Love the unconventional way you analyze and look at the world.
I Love that you live a committed sober lifestyle. I know how hard that must be and I admire your strength.
I Love that we have been friends for so long.

Love Celeste

Centered

Funky flair
But self-aware
She didn't dare
OMG that hair
She paints with every color

Aunt Dallas, Aunt Dallas
Your heart is the size of a Palace
A thousand rooms
But none for malice
You're centered like a ship's ballast

–Joel

Beaconesque

It was no fallacy
To watch Dallas feel the room,
With feelings showing
Brilliant, shining
Beaconesque;
She sought out across others
To capture & perfect
Even the tiniest feeling lurking there,
Under emotional veil.
Vulnerable, expressive,
This woman named after a city in Texas
Finds heaven
In a bubble bath.
Soft, floating, I see her
Smile showing in every shiny sphere
Supporting and floating gently
The beauty that is,
Was,
And will be. Dallas

–David

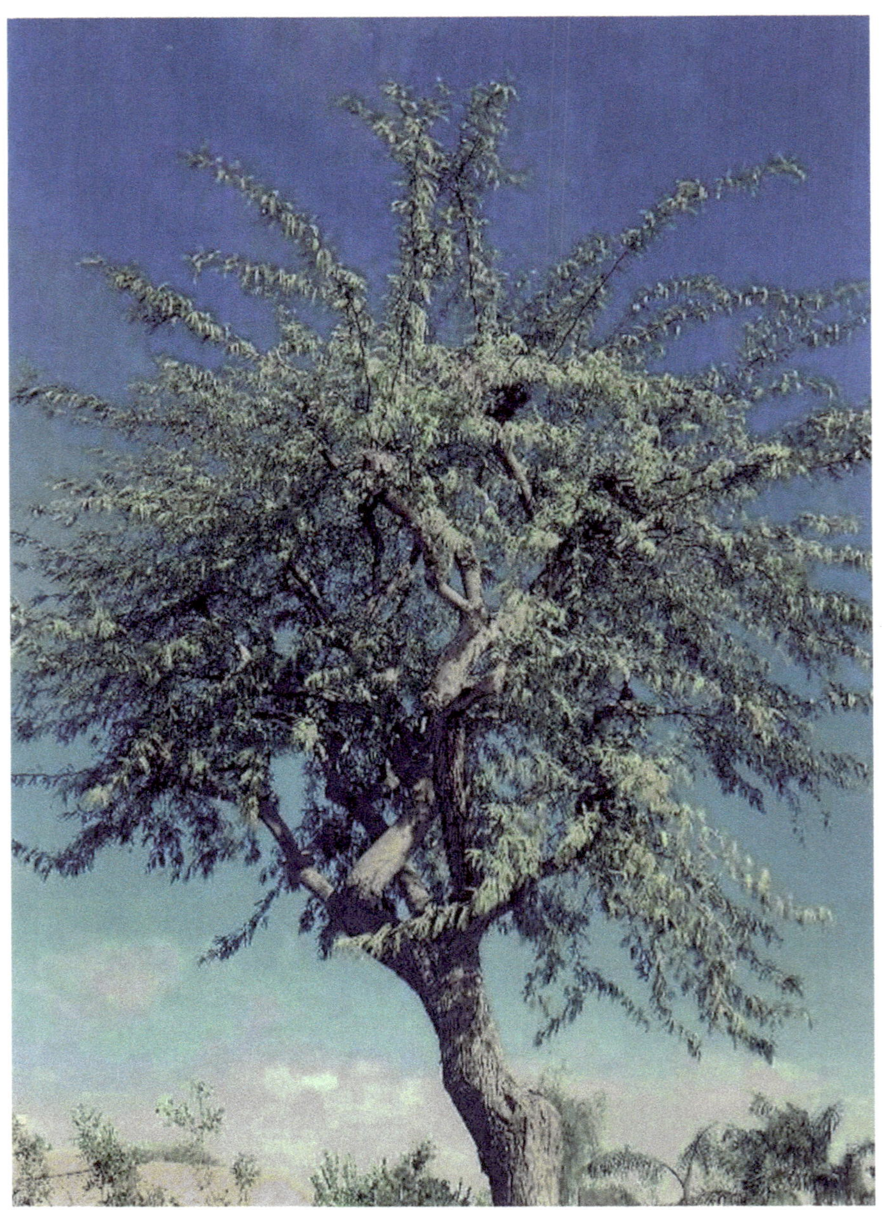

My Magical Tree

She stands out
among them all
sturdy and tall
roots so deep
my magical tree.

Her leaves change
she grows
with me
season by season
my magical tree.

Her long limbs
reach out
support me
year after year
my magical tree.

My Magical Tree (Continued)

She gives solace
a home
for me
Dallas O Dallas
my magical tree.

–Eileen

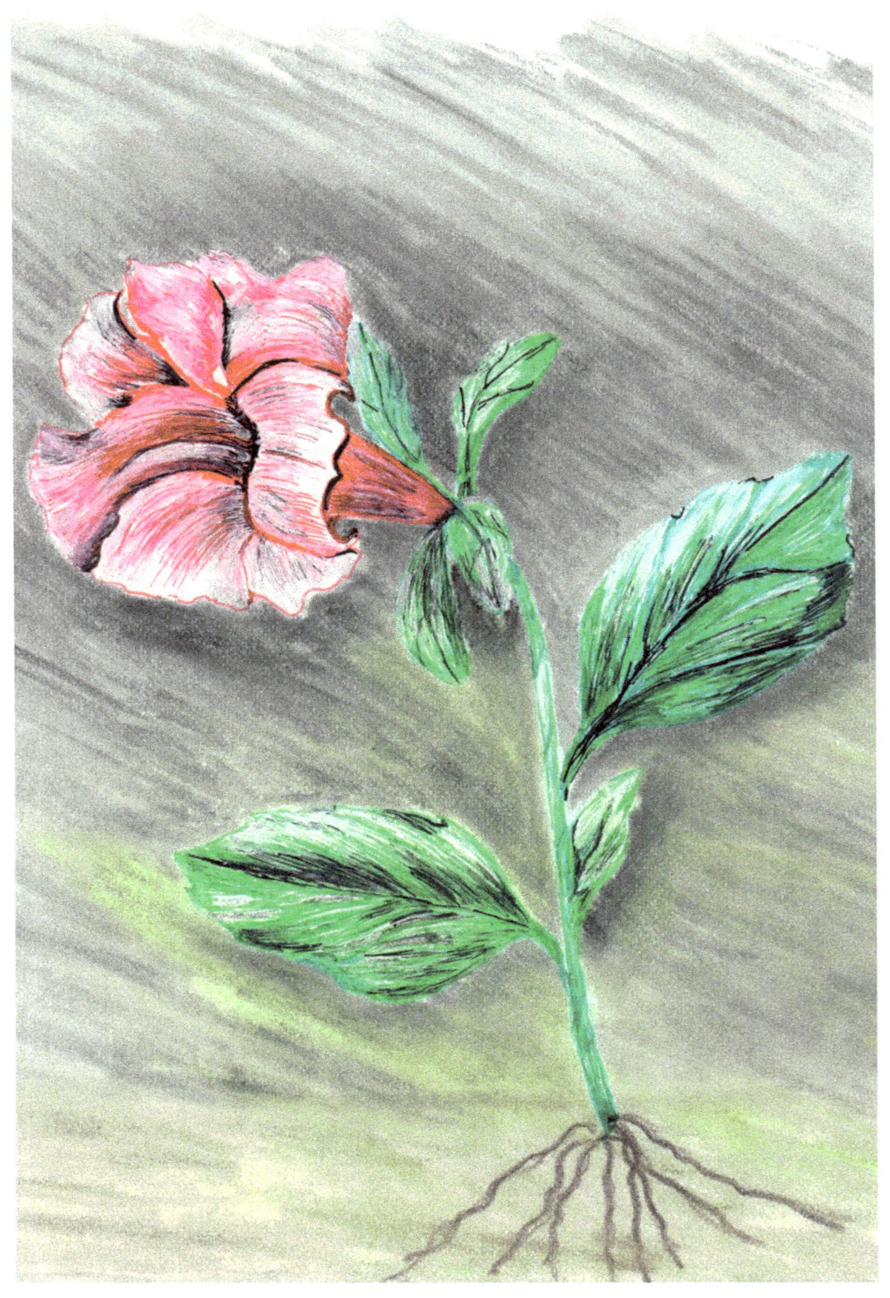

Chapter Fifteen

Grounded

Grounded

This is the end
Of Grounded,
The artwork
Of two friends

Dallas Ann
And Eileen
Their poetry
And drawings

Coming down
From the clouds
Roots abound
Underground

Through the years
What we've found
Is right here
On the ground

www.ingramcontent.com/pod-product-compliance
Lightning Source LLC
LaVergne TN
LVHW052344100826
845147LV00012B/750

9781954604995